Nayantara Sahgal is the author of several works of fiction and non-fiction, the first of which, *Prison and Chocolate Cake*, an autobiography, was published in 1954. Her works include classic novels such as *Rich Like Us*, *Plans for Departure* and *Lesser Breeds*. She has received the Sahitya Akademi Award, the Sinclair Prize and the Commonwealth Writers' Prize. Her novel, *When the Moon Shines by Day*, was longlisted for the 2018 JCB Prize. She returned her Sahitya Akademi Award in 2015 in protest against the murder by vigilantes of three writers, and the Akademi's silence at the time. She continues to be engaged in the ongoing protest against the assaults on the freedom of expression and democratic rights.

visionary of a romanticized village life, but he had seen in the early projects of community development in Etawa, Nilokheri and Faridabad a way to involve people in projects to improve their economic and socio-cultural conditions. The connection between this and the general development of the country was very clear to him when he said in 1957:

> It is the peasant who has borne the burden of India in ages past. It is on the growth and betterment of our peasantry that the future of India must necessarily depend.[30]

The Congress ministries in many provinces had tried to bring in tenancy reforms, an area of governance extremely tricky to navigate given the power structure of Indian politics and society. Nehru led from the front in 1950 by forcing the Zamindari Abolition Act through a constitutional amendment when the zamindars in many places like Bihar filled the courts with cases. One of the biggest changes was the amalgamation of the princely states into the larger political administration. This and the first election of 1952 would make this structural change a permanent feature in the villages. This would, in its train, bring about deep changes in village life. A researcher in a remote Gujarat village, Kasandra, for example, wrote in 1950 that it was as 'a period of radical transformation in the village and [among] its inhabitants. The period of radical transformation had begun with Independence in 1947...among the major

[30]Jawaharlal Nehru, 'Salt of the Earth', September 1957, *Kurukshetra*, Government of India, Delhi, 1961.

Nehru's India

Essays on the Maker of a Nation

Edited by

Nayantara Sahgal

SPEAKING TIGER

SPEAKING TIGER BOOKS LLP
125A, Ground Floor, Shahpur Jat, near Asiad Village,
New Delhi 110049

First published in hardback by
Speaking Tiger Publishing Pvt. Ltd. 2015

This edition first published in paperback by
Speaking Tiger Books 2022

ISBN: 978-93-5447-306-7
eISBN: 978-93-5447-312-8

'Nehru the Spiritualist' by Ramachandra Guha, p.75, was first published in *The Telegraph*, 15 November 2014, and is reproduced here with the kind permission of the author; 'Why Nehru Matters More Than Ever' by Neera Chandhoke, p.49, was first published in *The Hindu*, 8 August 2017, and is reproduced here with the kind permission of the author.

Photo on p.5 courtesy Wikimedia Commons.

10 9 8 7 6 5 4 3 2 1

Typeset in Bembo Roman by SÜRYA, New Delhi
Printed at Shree Maitrey Printech Pvt. Ltd., Noida

Mahatma Gandhi, Jawaharlal Nehru and Abul Kalam Azad,
Wardha, August 1935.

Contents

Introduction: Nehru's India: In Context 9
Nayantara Sahgal

Interpreting Nehru in the 21st Century 23
Mani Shankar Aiyar

Why Nehru Matters More Than Ever 49
Neera Chandhoke

Preserving the Ancient Palimpsest 55
Purushottam Agrawal

Nehru the Spiritualist 75
Ramachandra Guha

The Platonic Republican: Philosopher-Statesman 81
Kumar Ketkar

The Many Faces of Jawaharlal 103
Aakar Patel

The Truth-teller 115
Hartosh Bal

A Tryst with Nehru 129
Shiv Visvanathan

Nehru: The Homemaker 147
Rakesh Batabyal

The Indian Economy in the Nehru Era 167
Aditya Mukherjee and Mridula Mukherjee

Trustingly, JN 193
Gopalkrishna Gandhi

Remembering Nehru in the Dark Times 211
Shabnam Hashmi

My Quotidian Companion (The Common Man's Nehru) 223
Kiran Nagarkar

Panditji: Icon, Symbol, Emblem 249
Syeda Hameed

About the Contributors 266

Introduction

Nehru's India: In Context

This new edition of *Nehru's India* is especially welcome at this time. Since 2015 when it was first published, the Republic built by Nehru and his distinguished colleagues after Independence in 1947, which celebrated its diversity and secularism, has been under attack. Bringing Nehru's India back into focus was urgently needed.

The 'making of a nation' cannot quite convey the immensity and diversity of the enterprise undertaken by Jawaharlal Nehru that lifted a subcontinent out of political and economic serfdom and set it on the road to modernization. That this endeavour—starting with the brutal conditions confronting the first government of independent India—took place in an open society, without sacrificing individual freedom, made it the first of its kind in history.

In 1947 India was one of the world's poorest countries, impoverished by a century of plunder by Britain's East India Company, followed by a century of exploitation under the British Crown. Fifty percent of nearly four hundred million Indians lived below the poverty line. An economy designed for British enterprise and profit had halted indigenous growth. Such infrastructure as had been laid—roads, railways, telegraph wires—had served the needs of British industry and furthered British interests. Britain's wars in Europe and Asia had utilized Indian manpower and drained India's resources. The tax on land had been raised periodically to pay for the government's civil and military expenditure, thereby ruinously increasing rural indebtedness. The 1930s saw a series of famines, and during the Second World War, when grain was diverted to Britain's armies in war zones, the Bengal famine killed three million Indians. Independence itself brought the devastation of Partition. Some twelve million uprooted people were on the move across the subcontinent. Delhi was flooded with refugees. Like other parts of Delhi, the compound of the prime minister's house, then located at 17 York Road, was filled with tents to shelter the growing human tide.

Outside India great areas of Asia and Africa were still under European occupation and known as Europe's 'possessions'. The war had ended in 1945 but America's nuclear holocaust over Hiroshima and Nagasaki had ensured that mankind would never again be safe from the possibility of nuclear annihilation. The result was an escalating arms race, with the former wartime allies, the USA and the Soviet Union, locked in deadly competition for military superiority, and for control and influence across the globe. Post-war peace was a parody of peace that disguised a build-up towards another war, and it was aptly called the Cold War. At Independence, India faced a daunting and dangerous situation both at home and abroad.

The Indian National Congress that took power in 1947 had been led by Mahatma Gandhi since 1921. It was the first political formation—a national movement as much as a party—to demand independence from British rule and to build an organization to fight for it. Its countrywide reach gained an allegiance that flowed across region and religion, class and mass, language and gender. Its inclusiveness gave the movement its unique character, as did its creed of non-violence which brought women in their thousands to take part in its campaigns, court arrest and suffer imprisonment. Modern India's commitment to democracy, pluralism and equal status for all religions dates from this national experience. The political parties of the Hindu Right and the Muslim Right that based their identity on religion did not share this frame of mind and stayed out of the struggle for freedom. Its programme of law-breaking, defiance and imprisonment was not for the faint-hearted. And the courage demanded of those who confronted an empire's military might with satyagraha must have seemed to them nothing short of bizarre. During Nehru's twenty-six years of participation in the national movement—including nearly ten spent in jails—the country had come to know him better, and he had come to know Indians better, than any political figure apart from Gandhi. He had travelled all over the country, spoken and written extensively about his views on a variety of subjects, and shared the significance of events in India and abroad with rural and urban, educated and unlettered audiences. The relationship that had grown out of these encounters was one of mutual trust, and of faith in each other. It was the only one of its kind in political India and it has remained the only one of its kind.

Nehru was a socialist. In our blinkered market-obsessed climate socialism is taboo. But a free run of capitalism would have been grossly out of touch with Indian and world realities in Nehru's day. The best minds—in politics, economics, history, art, literature and theatre—understood socialism as the economic approach best suited to serve humanity's needs. Not least, it represented the most civilized human instincts. Nehru's socialism was free of dogma and doctrine. He described his approach to economic development as 'experimental' and 'flexible'. It could not be otherwise in what he called the uncharted territory he was treading. In a dire economic situation he looked for professional guidance. It came from Indian specialists, statisticians, and scientists, and also, interestingly, from an American engineer, Dr Solomon Trone, who was known for his wide and varied experience. The General Electric Company had sent Trone to the Soviet Union during India's first Five Year Plan period and he had helped to build the Dnieper Dam. He had been industrial advisor to Chiang Kai Shek's government in China and to the government of Japan. Invited by Nehru to India, Trone urged immediate and drastic action, starting with a national plan under Nehru's personal supervision. He also urged Nehru to act in consultation with the best brains in the country, as President Roosevelt had done during America's worst economic crisis. Among the areas he identified to be taken up immediately were additional steel plants, electricity generating equipment and a machine tools industry. His suggestions figured in the first two Five Year Plans. The scale and immense range of development, based on a public sector, a private sector, and a joint sector, has been widely documented. Irrigation projects, research laboratories, agricultural universities, IITs (Indian Institutes of Technology), and steel mills (with collaboration from Britain, Germany and the Soviet Union) laid the foundations for industrial, agricultural and scientific transformation.

At a time when the world's judgmental eyes were watching India, contemporary assessments of India's economic development by informed foreign observers are of special interest because they tell us exactly the opposite of what today's critics say, that the economic direction the country took under Nehru was a mistake. The first Plan's priority had been agriculture, and fertilizer production made its mark on it. Percival Griffiths, retired from the ICS (Indian Civil Service), and sceptical of India's capabilities, wrote that foodgrain production since Independence had been 'spectacular', and that India had succeeded in doing what many observers including himself had regarded as impossible.[1]

Griffiths observed: 'It is impossible to travel round India today without feeling that the country has entered

---

[1]Sir Percival Griffiths, *Modern India*, Ernest Benn Ltd., London, 1957, p.207.

a new, dynamic phase...in the villages...the signs of a rise in the standard of living are unmistakable.'[2]

Michael Brecher, Nehru's biographer, called the first Five Year Plan 'an unquestioned success. Food production reached a new high...'[3]

In his detailed account of the successes and failures of the first two Plans, he concludes: 'Having said all this, it remains to be emphasized that India's progress is most impressive, measured both against its own previous conditions and against the record of any other underdeveloped country which has chosen the democratic route to social and economic change. No less vital is the point, which cannot be overstressed, that whatever progress has been achieved is primarily due to the efforts of the prime minister. Indeed he is the heart and soul and mind of India's heroic struggle to raise the living standards of its 390 million people.'[4]

Barbara Ward comes to much the same positive conclusion in her assessment of the Plans: 'What is happening is a process of continuous growth under broad government stimulus and guidance...in the private sector, the executive function is as wide as Indian enterprise and covers everything from Tata's works at Jamshedpur, producing over half a million tons of steel a year, down to the villager selling his first maund of rice in the market...[5] Never has private enterprise

---

[2]Griffiths, pp.205-6.

[3]Michael Brecher, *Nehru: A Political Biography*, OUP, London, 1959, p.526.

[4]Brecher, p.553.

[5]Barbara Ward, *India and the West*, Hamish Hamilton, London, 1961, p.145.

expanded or diversified so quickly as in the last decade. Its investment in all sectors, including agriculture, almost doubled between the first and second Plans...[6] In spite of some difficulties and disappointments, the Indian record in both infrastructure and industry is one of substantial advance on a broad front, amounting to something very like the "big push" needed to achieve sustained growth.'[7]

The cooperation of government and people, the palpable involvement of the men and women working at local levels, and the mood of shared adventure that inspired a surge of national effort, led by Nehru's single-minded commitment to it, were apparent to India-watchers at this time. In his study of Nehru's first ten years in power, Vincent Sheean writes: 'Nobody wants to exaggerate the changes that have set in...but we should be deaf and blind, as well as a little stupid, not to perceive that change is afoot...Here, too, we encounter the fact that Nehru has been the prime mover...The keenness of the young, the national movement of hope...is sustained by his [Nehru's] presence. I have yet to see any work, plant, enterprise, school, hospital or laboratory which he has not visited.'[8] Newsreels of the time show Nehru at these sites, listening and learning, keeping abreast of developments, thrusting into crowds, running up flights of stairs. Nehru was a man in a hurry. The country

---

[6]Ward, pp.159, 161.

[7]Ward, p.172.

[8]Vincent Sheean, *Nehru: The Years of Power*, Random House, New York, 1960, pp.69-70.

responded. From a condition of zero percent growth during 1900-47, the first fifteen years of independence (until the Chinese attack in 1962) saw the economy grow to four percent, bringing India in line with the successful economies of the time, and ahead of China, Japan and the UK.[9]

Science was crucial to Nehru's concept of a modern nation, and to the making of the modern mind. An atomic reactor set up in Bombay attained criticality in 1956. The successful mission to Mars in 2013-14 celebrated an achievement that had been built on scientific progress since Independence. Another foreign observer saw more to Nehru's India than measureable progress. One of the twentieth century's leading scientists, J.B.S. Haldane of Britain, emigrated with his wife, also a scientist, to India in 1957 and took Indian citizenship. This he did not only because of Nehru's commitment to train young minds in science, but because—as he told the Oxford University Socialist Club in January 1956—'One has the absolute impression of being in a highly civilized community...I feel far more at home there than I do in some European and most American cities.'

The contrast between the Nehru era and now is vivid. The present government whose repeated refrain is development, seems to regard it as a process divorced from nature, environment and the needs and rights of human beings.

Nehru's foreign policy is another focus of criticism.

---

[9]Pulapri Balakrishnan, *Economic Growth in India: History and Prospect*, OUP, Delhi, pp.56 and 58-59.

Yet more than any other factor, it proclaimed India's birth into independent nationhood and independence of judgment. Non-alignment was a master stroke. By providing a platform for Afro-Asian cooperation—joined by Tito's Yugoslavia—it led to a historic shift of power and perspective in a Eurocentric world. Powerless new nations entered the halls of decision-making and became a combine to be reckoned with at the United Nations (UN). Their refusal to take sides in the Cold War or to join military pacts and blocs left them free to make their own decisions. Nehru's international awareness had, in fact, given the Congress a far-sighted foreign policy long before Independence. The party had declared its support for Abyssinia when it was under bombardment and occupation by Italy, and had sent a medical mission to war-torn China. Nehru himself had taken a passionate stand—years ahead of his political contemporaries in Europe—against fascism and Nazism—and had made common cause with countries fighting colonial rule. The two Asian Relations Conferences held in Delhi immediately before and after Independence brought the region's countries together for the first time. India's ongoing support at the UN for a Palestinian state and for the grim struggle against apartheid in South Africa were a continuation of the voice Nehru had repeatedly raised against inhuman policies.

Peace—so sorely needed for development—was the prime objective of Nehru's foreign policy and he took the lead in pursuing it (apart from non-alignment) through active cooperation with the UN in solutions to end war. India took the chairmanship of the Commission to repatriate Korean prisoners of war, worked for a settlement in Indo-China after Ho Chi Minh's victory over the French, and sent Indian troops to the Gaza strip and the Congo for the UN's peace-keeping operations. The trustworthy reputation India enjoys at the UN and in international affairs was built by foreign policy under Nehru.

Integral to the pursuit of peace were his efforts to seat the People's Republic of China in its rightful place at the UN, as successor to Nationalist China which had been a founder-member of the organization. It was obvious that isolating an established government because it was communist would make for confrontation and conflict, as it already had during the Korean War. But isolating communism was central to America's Cold War strategy. India had recognized the new Chinese government on 30 December 1949. It took America another thirty years to acknowledge the importance of China in world affairs. Meanwhile the long arm of the Cold War took its heavy toll in Tibet. In 1959 a CIA-aided armed rebellion orchestrated an uprising in Lhasa that ended in the slaughter of thousands of Tibetans. Thousands more were forced to flee to India with the Dalai Lama. China was convinced the uprising was part of an international conspiracy to destabilize its government and that India, having given asylum to the Dalai Lama, had been party to it. The Chinese government took a hostile turn towards India. Claims to large tracts of Indian territory followed, and ultimately the Chinese attack in 1962.

Much has been written about where the responsibility

lies for this China-India border conflict. An original reading of it by the Tibetan historian, Tsering Shakya, is significant against the background of the Cold War which waged its proxy wars over Europe, Asia and Africa. Tsering Shakya writes: '...from the Chinese point of view the American involvement in Tibet transformed the entire situation. It was no longer a question of revolt by some troublesome Tibetans but an international conspiracy to undermine the victory of the Communist Party in China. Moreover, it presented a direct threat to China's security.'[10] He goes on to say: 'If it had not been for the Tibetan revolt, the border issue (between India and China) would have been confined to a diplomatic exchange of notes.'[11]

According to this analysis, China and India may well have lived with their differences, or inched along to some form of agreement—given India's policy of strict non-interference in the Tibetan issue, and Mao's assurance to the young Dalai Lama in 1954, that Tibet would enjoy an autonomy that no other Chinese province was allowed—had it not been for America's disastrous covert intervention in Tibet, leading to the border war in India.

A word about the Cold War: Europe has been at war against Europe for centuries—over territory, over religion, over colonial rivalry, and most recently (joined by the United States) in the name of ideology. Its

[10]Tsering Shakya, *The Dragon in the Land of Shadows: A History of Modern Tibet Since 1947*, Penguin Compass, New York, 2001, p.171.

[11]Tsering Shakya, p.281.

proxy wars have raged over Korea, Laos, the Congo, Vietnam, Central Europe and Afghanistan. The secret services of the superpowers have provided rich material for spy fiction, films and folklore. (A Hollywood film, *Full Metal Jacket*, has a scene showing American troops in training for war in Vietnam chanting 'Ho Chi Minh is a son-of-a-bitch' in time to their rhythmic jogging.) No surprise, then, that Tibet added one more killing field to the Cold War's bloody battlegrounds. There is certainly reason to wonder whether, without American interference, Tibetans would have been granted more autonomy than elsewhere in China, the Dalai Lama would not have had to flee Tibet, and India would have been spared a humiliating defeat in a war that discredited an enlightened foreign policy.

Political leadership has its successes and failures. It is a strength of democracy that leaders are taken to task for their failures, as Nehru was for the collapse of his China policy. It is also true—though rare in the annals of politics—that human quality transcends political leadership and reaches across political divisions and differences. Nehru's prime ministership was admired worldwide as an era of heroic striving against gigantic odds, with no curtailment of the rights and freedoms guaranteed to all Indians. On Nehru's death, Adlai Stevenson's tribute summed up this view: 'He was one of God's great creations in our time. His monument is his nation and his dream of freedom and of ever-expanding well-being for all men.'

In the Lok Sabha, a Jan Sangh MP, Atal Bihari

Vajpayee's words reflected deep mourning: '...a dream has remained half-fulfilled, a song has become silent...like Ram, Nehru was the orchestrator of the impossible and the inconceivable...he too was not afraid of compromise but would never compromise under duress...the leader has gone but the followers remain. The sun has set, yet by the shadow of stars we must find our way.'[12]

Asked how he would like to be remembered, Nehru had composed a singularly unpolitical epitaph for himself: 'This was a man who with all his mind and heart loved India and the Indian people. And they in turn were indulgent to him and gave him their love most abundantly and extravagantly.'[13]

Nehru's legacy has so far stood the test of time. Secularism is part of Indian culture, and elections based on adult suffrage have given rise to a canny electorate well aware of its importance. But this inheritance is now under attack. The BJP (Bharatiya Janata Party) government of Rajasthan decreed in 2015 that candidates for election to panchayats must have an educational (Class VIII) qualification and specified toilet arrangements at home. Here begins the stealthy subversion of democracy and its institutions. The RSS (Rashtriya Swayamsevak Sangh) clamours for a Hindu rashtra and a re-write of history that will disown centuries of Indian civilization, while its assaults on other religions and other points of view have left millions of Indians in fear for their future. Mythology and fantasy parade as knowledge, with what

---

[12]Blog posted by Ramachandra Guha.

[13]Quoted in *The Statesman*, 21 January 1954.

extent of damage to facts and reason we cannot tell. Nazi rule in Germany showed us how fragile facts can become when they are repeatedly battered out of shape. We now see that not only Nehru's legacy, but Nehru himself is being brazenly written out of history. In Indonesia to mark the sixtieth anniversary of the Bandung conference of 1955, the Indian envoy chose to omit his name altogether, along with the fact that Nehru pioneered Afro-Asian unity and was a founder of the Non-Aligned Movement at Bandung.

The rising tide of India's brand of fascism now endangers the inheritance we celebrate as the Idea of India, and makes it necessary to resurrect Nehru's role in building and safeguarding it. This collection of assessments, criticisms, opinions, insights and emotions tells us how his contribution is viewed five decades after his death. Common to all of them is one hard fact: No Nehru, no modern India. The ground we stand on was laid in Nehru's time. One essayist calls for political activism as the need of the hour to protect what we prize as India's legacy. Meanwhile the battle is on between enlightenment and obscurantism, between Nehru's vision of India and the BJP/RSS's shrunken and distorted version of India.

Dehradun,
September 2022

Nayantara Sahgal

Interpreting Nehru in the 21st Century

Mani Shankar Aiyar

A Personal Introduction

I was born in 1941 and was six when Jawaharlal Nehru became prime minister. He died when I was twenty-three, a few days after he saw a bunch of us foreign service probationers emerging out of the basement of the ministry where we were being given our training in cyphers, and, somewhat to our chagrin, heard him quizzically enquire, '*Yeh bachche kaun hain*?' It was the only time I encountered him face-to-face.

So, I grew from infancy through adolescence to adulthood knowing only one prime minister, a prime minister it was impossible to consider anyone replacing. He permeated our thinking on virtually every aspect of our lives; so, growing up was growing with him. Around the age of sixteen, I was introduced to his

Autobiography,[1] then, a little later, to his *Discovery of India*,[2] a voyage to discover what it meant for me to be an Indian. His *Glimpses of World History*[3] became an invaluable source of reference. About the time I entered college, Michael Brecher published Nehru's biography, and the chapter most discussed among us was 'The Duumvirate', as a kind of 'compare and contrast' Nehru with Sardar Patel. It was also the period that saw the publication of Nehru's *A Bunch of Old Letters*,[4] and we were able to live with him through his tempestuous alliance with Subhas Chandra Bose—a relationship of profound consequence for our understanding of the ethical dimensions of the Freedom Movement. These are all books revisited over the years as the significance of the words expands with every re-reading. And although Nehru passed away in my early youth, to me he still remains the ultimate mentor, the definitive influence on my worldview and India's place in that world. I recall with wry amusement Rajiv Gandhi presenting me a watch on Nehru's birth centenary which had a picture of him on the face, and saying, 'You're always thinking of him; now you can also see him all the time!'

---

[1]Jawaharlal Nehru, *An Autobiography: Towards Freedom*, first published by Bodley Head, UK, 1936.

[2]Jawaharlal Nehru, *The Discovery of India*, first published by OUP, New Delhi, 1946.

[3]Jawaharlal Nehru, *Glimpses of World History*, first published in two volumes, 1934-35, Kitabistan, Allahabad; reissued by the Jawaharlal Nehru Memorial Fund, 1982, eighteenth edition pub. 2003.

[4]Jawaharlal Nehru, *A Bunch of Old Letters*, first published by Asia Publishing House, 1958; reissued by Penguin Books India, 2005.

What did I take away from all this? One was the complete absence of egoism in the man's writings. Whereas most autobiographies are about 'I, me, myself', Jawaharlal as a person is marginal to his story; it is his thoughts that permeate the narrative. His *Autobiography*, the historian Rudrangshu Mukherjee notes, was marked by 'doubt and ambiguity'. He preferred the 'shade of grey. His comments were open-ended and nuanced. There was self-criticism and self-scrutiny'.[5]

Second, the ethical dimension to politics: an obsessive concern with ends and means, the conviction that only right means can lead to right ends. As Michael Brecher put it, a tithe cruelly, if Sardar Patel was a 'man of action', Nehru was a 'man of right action'. Commenting on Mahatma Gandhi's remark that 'Jawahar is a thinker, Sardar a doer', Brecher concedes that 'Nehru must certainly be classified as a "thinker". But Jawaharlal has always been a man of action for whom thought is primarily the key to *right action*' (italics in the original).[6]

And, third, that oratory must be leavened by regard for the truth. This is perhaps best illustrated in the opening lines of Nehru's famous 'Tryst with Destiny' speech. He begins: 'Long years ago, we made a tryst with destiny and now the time comes when we shall redeem our pledge…' To end there would have been perfect oratory. But because Nehru was a stickler for

---

[5]Rudrangshu Mukherjee, *Nehru & Bose: Parallel Lives*, Penguin/Viking, India, 2014, p.133.

[6]Michael Brecher, *Nehru: A Political Biography*, OUP, New Delhi, 1959, Chapter XV, 'The Duumvirate', pp.392-93.

the truth, the conditionality is introduced '...not wholly, nor in full measure, but very substantially'.

Much has happened in the intervening years to filter adulation through critical appraisal. But, at the end of the day, whatever reservations one might have about this or that event in his stewardship of the nation, and particularly of the sad end that followed the India-China armed conflict of 1962, he remains the 'Gentle Colossus' of Hiren Mukherjee's memoir.[7]

That he achieved this influence on the imagination of India while remaining a committed democrat is perhaps his most enduring achievement. For others have achieved equal eminence but usually by blotting out their rivals and imposing themselves. Nehru was voluntarily accepted, both by his ardent followers and his many trenchant critics. I was eighteen when his government dismissed the first elected communist government, E.M.S. Namboodiripad's in Kerala. Someone secured passes for the debate in Parliament. It was my first time in the Visitors' Gallery. Spellbound, I heard Comrade Dange denounce Nehru as he sat impassive opposite, deeply attentive through the speech. Dange ended with a peroration in which he compared Nehru to Yudhishtir who won a major battle in the *Mahabharata* by pronouncing a white lie. In consequence, his chariot that always rode above the earth for his never telling a lie, fell to the ground. Pointing to Nehru, Dange said his chariot too had now fallen to the ground. He was

[7]Hiren Mukherjee, *The Gentle Colossus*, Manisha Granthalaya, Kolkata, 1964.

listened to in complete silence; then Nehru rose to reply. I remember nothing of Nehru's reply—but the image graven in my memory is of his listening with profound care to the cascade of criticism poured on him. There have been few leaders of his stature who have demonstrated such abiding respect for democratic dissidence and democratic practice.

Another key instance of Nehru as a democrat occurred in the middle of the 1962 war with China. Soon after Tawang fell, Atal Bihari Vajpayee, then all of thirty-six years old and leader of a party of just four MPs (Members of Parliament), called on the prime minister to request him to convene the Rajya Sabha to debate the course of the war. Nehru promptly agreed. On 8 November, young Vajpayee opened the debate with a searing indictment of Nehru's foreign and defence policies. The debate was allowed, indeed encouraged, to roll to its end. In contrast, when a demand was made for the convening of the Rajya Sabha during the Kargil war of 1999, Vajpayee, now prime minister, declined to summon the House into session.

The Four Pillars of Nehruvian Thought

The four key dimensions of India's modern nationhood, as conceived and implemented by Jawaharlal Nehru, were: Democracy; Secularism; Socialism; and Non-alignment. They were interpreted by Nehru in the light of our requirements, as he saw them, in the mid-twentieth century, that is, in the aftermath of the horrors of Partition and in the glow of the first few years of

Independence. As national compulsions altered, the interpretation of these four dimensions also underwent change—change to the point where these came to be either distorted beyond recognition or abandoned altogether. Indeed, at times and in some quarters, their continuing relevance also came under challenge. What needs examination is whether five decades after he passed away, these are still the defining parameters of India's contemporary nationhood and, if so, how they should be interpreted in the light of present circumstances.

Democracy

Democracy is clearly an unalterable dimension. There is no serious challenge to this, perhaps because those who would prefer a more authoritarian form of government have been kept sufficiently far from the centre of power to entertain no more than pipe dreams. That, however, is changing with the ascent to power of the saffron forces in May 2014. As they have reached where they have through the electoral route, and at least so long as they continue on a high electoral trajectory, they are likely to remain democratic. If they slip, they might be tempted to consider an alternative route but that, at present at any rate, appears unlikely. So, the Constitution, our fundamental rights thereunder, Parliament and the state assemblies, an independent judiciary, and a free media, appear to have come to stay. However, we have got so used to the fact of being a democracy that it often escapes our attention as to what a miracle this has been. For, of approximately 150 nations that have come to liberation of one kind or another since 1947, ours is almost the only one, and certainly the only one of such size and diversity, to have not only forged a democracy but to have sustained it over seventy-five years. Of course, the Emergency was a major deviation, but even that dark period was proclaimed under the Constitution, and validated by the Supreme Court, as also removed under the provisions of the same Constitution. The danger is that there is an inherent fragility in the achievement in view of its not having proved replicable, at least on a sustained basis, anywhere in our neighbourhood or around the world. Therefore, we cannot be complacent—but we can be confident that, barring an unlikely catastrophe, we will, as a nation, succeed in persisting on the democratic path, provided we remain ever vigilant and, as a people, resist authoritarianism when it rears its ugly head.

Thus, by insisting on a democratic polity and 'nurturing it like a mother nurtures her child', as Sonia Gandhi remarked at Nehru's 125th birth anniversary celebration, Nehru established the democratic ethos, the democratic institutions and the democratic practices that other powerful leaders of newly independent countries found so easy to abandon. We did indeed become the 'world's largest democracy'. But because Mahatma Gandhi's wise counsel was pushed to one side immediately after he was assassinated, the Constitution facilitated democratic institutions in Delhi and the state capitals, on the model of Westminster and Capitol Hill, with a few features borrowed from other countries, but remained quintessentially, to quote Dr B.R. Ambedkar, 'a Union of States'. Institutions of local self-government, without which there can be 'representative democracy' but not '*participatory* democracy', were initially left entirely out of the purview of the Draft Constitution but subsequently allowed to survive on the margins of the Constitution, in a paragraph of just four lines in the Directive Principles, as the remnant of an eccentric Gandhian view of the Constitution. In Gandhi's conception, encapsulated in a 1946 publication, *A Gandhian Constitution for Independent India* by Shriman Narayan Agarwal,[8] fulsomely validated and endorsed by the Mahatma himself in his Introduction, elected village panchayats were to be the very foundation of the Constitution. Indeed, Gandhiji went so far as to suggest that village panchayats be the basic 'units' of democracy, direct elections with universal suffrage being held only at the village level; higher echelons of the system, at state and national level, being elected indirectly by the immediately lower level. In today's idiom, Gandhiji had foreseen the role of 'money-and-muscle power' in distorting the representative nature of the democratic polity. However, Dr Ambedkar insisted that the individual, not the village community, must be the basic unit of democracy, and denigrated villages as being 'cesspools' and, therefore, unqualified for democracy without safeguards for the scheduled castes and tribes. But, by thus casting off elected community institutions, Ambedkar did not answer the question of how to make our democracy participatory on a

[8]Pub. Kitabistan, Allahabad, 1946.

continuous basis, instead of the individual having little role in governance beyond the right to vote once every five years. He also did not address the conundrum of the Westminster model being based on constituencies with an average voting population of about 30,000 while in India it stretches for Parliament from 1.5 million to over two million. The United Kingdom, in consequence, has one hundred MPs *more* than the Lok Sabha, with an electorate that is one-twentieth the Indian size, besides being backed by a plethora of well-established local bodies ranging from the parish to the county councils to the boroughs and the metropolitan corporations—older and, therefore, stronger than Parliament in their designated spheres—to meet the daily requirements of the populace. The reconciliation of a distant representative democracy with the imperative of a neighbourhood participatory democracy was thus left unresolved in the Constitution adopted in 1950. That task was left to state governments to proceed with or not.

Nehru kept himself out of the argument. There is a passing reference in the closing pages of his *The Discovery of India* to the village as a basic unit but he took no active part in the debate between the Gandhians and the Ambedkarites over Panchayati Raj. But very soon into the development process he found that rural governance was a gaping lacuna in the system adopted on Republic Day 1950. He thought he had found an answer in community development, espoused principally by S.K. Dey, Minister for Cooperation and Panchayati Raj, with assistance from an American precedent, but found within a decade that while community development had spawned a vast rural bureaucracy, it little involved the people in decision-making on planning or implementation. The mass of the people remained as removed from governance as before we had become a fully representative democracy. In language used decades later by his grandson, Rajiv Gandhi, India was, indeed, the world's 'largest democracy' but also the 'least representative'. Therefore, the veteran Gandhian, Balvantray Mehta (who later went on to become chief minister of Gujarat) was commissioned to head a Study Group that recommended at the fag end of 1957 that a three-tier system of Panchayati Raj be introduced all over rural India to bring the masses into the processes of governance. The enthusiasm with which Nehru embraced this concept left his principal biographer, Dr S. Gopal,[9] a little bewildered by Nehru's 'magnificent obsession' but it did give the country seven years of spreading democracy downwards and outwards over the whole land. Tragically, with Nehru's death in 1964, Panchayati Raj withered on the vine. Rajiv analysed the cause as the result of Panchayati Raj having been left to state legislation instead of being given Constitutional status, sanction and sanctity.

Such Constitutional safeguards and more have been accorded to Panchayati Raj since the amendments of 1993, the longest and most detailed amendments ever, now incorporated in the Constitution as Part IX ('The Panchayats') and Part IXA ('The Municipalities'), thus

[9]Sarvepalli Gopal, *Jawaharlal Nehru: A Biography*, Vol. I, 1889-1947; Vol. II, 1947-1956; Vol. III, 1956-1964, OUP, New Delhi, 2004.

rendering Panchayati Raj ineluctable, irremovable and irreversible. We now have close to 2,50,000 rural and urban institutions of local self-government to which we have elected no less than 3.2 million representatives, of whom nearly 1.3 million are women. The scheduled castes and tribes (and in many states the Other Backward Classes or OBCs) are represented at every level in proportion to their population at that level. Equally, there are around 80,000 scheduled caste/scheduled tribe presidents of panchayats and close to one lakh women presidents at all three tiers. We thus have more elected women in India than in the rest of the world put together! This is an achievement without precedent in history or parallel in the contemporary world. We have made India not only the world's largest democracy but also the world's most representative democracy.

Yet the achievement remains unsung because the panchayats have been left empty shells without real power or authority in many states. In some states, there has indeed been a significant measure of empowerment, and there has been some progress in all states, but after nearly a quarter century of the passage of the amendments, Panchayati Raj remains a largely incomplete story. Completing that story by ensuring that panchayats and urban local bodies, and most particularly their community assemblies in gram sabhas and ward sabhas, are genuinely empowered to make their own lives, and control their own destinies, is the great unfinished Nehruvian task before democracy in the twenty-first century.

Secularism

Nehruvian secularism faces challenges in the twenty-first century that are in many ways the same as he faced but in some significant respects different. The massacres and displacements of Partition had placed before the nation the stark choice of becoming, like Pakistan, a state based on religion, or retaining our composite heritage as a secular country for all our people, whatever their religion. Nehru, and most Indians, chose secularism. But a significant minority remained proponents of Hindu Mahasabha (HMS) president Veer Savarkar's 'Hindutva', a word translated by Savarkar himself as 'Hindudom', with the same implications as 'Christendom', that is, Hindu Rule. Little wonder that Savarkar publicly endorsed Muhammad Ali Jinnah's two-nation theory in a speech in Nagpur on 15 August 1943. In this construct, a Muslim Pakistan made a Hindu India even more imperative. This widened and deepened the rift between the concept of a Hindu India and that of a secular India. It remains, seventy-five years into independence, as the unbridgeable divide between most Indians and some Indians. At Independence, the Muslim minority had to be reassured that India would be home to all, notwithstanding Partition. Jawaharlal summed up this approach in a single sentence at a gathering in the Ram Lila grounds on Gandhi Jayanti, 1951: 'If anyone raises his hand against another in the name of religion, I shall fight him till the last breath of my life, whether from inside the government or outside.'[10]

---

[10]*Hindustan Times*, 4 October 1951.

That point has since been made but the rise of Hindutva to political power, largely by suppressing but not eliminating the Hindutva element from their political platform, poses a far subtler challenge to those who espouse secularism as not only a political construct but as quintessentially a way of life.

With Hindutva made into an ulterior rather than overt political objective, secular India should not be relieved but remain vigilant. The Hindutva agenda was not politically convenient at election time but as the Sangh Parivar is clearly involving itself in all aspects of government and governance, and as Hindutva remains the ideological anchor of the BJP (Bharatiya Janata Party), the saffron forces are merely awaiting their Godhra[11] moment to bring their real agenda into focus. For the secularists to lower their guard at this juncture, as some are inclined to do, and become complacent that the leopard has changed its spots would be quite the wrong approach to take. Our secularism should be on red alert. This is the moment not so much for cerebral secularism—arguing the pros and cons of secularism—as for secular activism—being ready at a moment's notice to rush to hotspots as soon as they arise without waiting for communal incidents to become a spreading rash. This calls for the revival by the Congress of its Sadbhavana Sena that appears to have died with the

[11]The torching of a railway carriage in which Hindu pilgrims were travelling, at Godhra, Gujarat, which triggered the 2002 Gujarat violence in which, according to official estimates, 800 Muslims were killed though human rights campaigners claim the number was several times higher.

untimely death of its first chairman, Sunil Dutt. It was nowhere to be seen when Saharanpur went up in flames; it was not present at Trilokpuri or Bawana. We need highly trained activists who, in the manner of a Rapid Action Force, will rush to the scene as soon as trouble is scented. Politically too, there needs to be promoted a one-point secular front that is as active in Parliament as it should be outside.

Lastly, those who suggest ducking as the appropriate response to the charge of 'appeasement' should not be heeded. The Justice Rajinder Sachar committee (appointed in 2005 by then Prime Minister Manmohan Singh) has convincingly established that while equal rights to the Muslim minority have been constitutionally guaranteed, at several levels the community is seriously disadvantaged. It is disadvantaged in terms of feeling under siege by those who deride their efforts to remain themselves; they are disadvantaged in terms of their sense of personal security; they are disadvantaged in terms of economic, educational and social progress as a community. Special, focused action is required to deal with such community-level disadvantage. The Constitution allows for affirmative action. Such action must be taken without fear or favour. The integration of the Muslim community into the mainstream of Indian life is a work in progress of key importance to the integrity of the nation. Faltering because we might be accused of *tushtikaran* (appeasement) amounts to letting down fifteen crore of our fellow-citizens. Any fears that the majority community might entertain about such action needs to be patiently explained in terms of how such steps do not disadvantage the Hindu but merely restore the balance of advantage. We must end the salience in some minds between Pakistan and Indian Muslims. They are a precious part of India's life and heritage, who have consciously decided to throw in their lot with our country when they had the choice of finding another home across the border.

Socialism

Socialism and planning as the centre-piece of the Congress party's economic platform goes back to the Karachi Congress of 1931. That was the consequence of the socialist ginger group put together by Nehru, with Subhas Bose as his principal companion-in-arms. But this was more the climax of Nehru's own economic thinking than its commencement. For his radicalization began with what was initially a chance encounter with peasants' issues in the Allahabad-Lucknow belt in the early 1920s, followed by his 1926-27 stay in Europe where he attended a meeting of the League Against Imperialism in Brussels, where he met a number of European socialists and, more significantly, the Chinese revolutionary delegation. He also briefly visited the Soviet Union as an official guest at the tenth anniversary celebrations of their 'October Revolution'. Impressed as he was by the outstanding economic achievements of the burgeoning Soviet Union, yet his abhorrence at their methods also came through. Later, he was to write in his autobiography: 'Communists often irritated me by their dictatorial ways, their aggressive and rather vulgar methods, their habit of denouncing everybody who did not agree with them.'[12]

But it was on his return to India that he started evolving a very Indian brand of 'socialism' in reaction to, and in opposition to, both the innate conservatism of his seniors in the Congress party and in contradistinction to the Gandhian formula for economic reform. The conservatives thought little about economic issues and, when they did, were inclined to leave economic and social relations as they were. On the other hand, starting from his 1909 *Hind Swaraj* reflections, Gandhi had radical ideas of reforming Indian society and the economy but these were less concerned with class conflicts, in the Marxian sense, than with empowering village communities to be self-reliant and, to the maximum extent possible, self-reliant within a democratic framework. He also took Indian poverty as a given, and wanted the individual to adjust himself to the reality, but rising morally to the challenge of restraining wants and catering to the needs of the even more needy. While Nehru was to return to many Gandhian ideas in later life, particularly after the publication in 1957 of the Balvantray Mehta Study Group report on Panchayati Raj, as the 1920s turned to the 1930s Nehru increasingly elaborated his plans for a radical transformation of the Indian economy, beginning with the abolition of zamindari and accelerating industrialization through the planning process which would place the state at the

[12]Cited by Judith Brown, *Nehru: A Political Life*, OUP, New Delhi, 2003, p.82.

commanding heights of the Indian economy. Inspired though this programme was by the Soviet example, it rejected the regimentation of society and the brutal dictatorship that increasingly characterized Stalin's system. It was an India-specific model of socialism that Nehru evolved in his mind and educated the party into accepting. He described this in the following terms at the 1928 Bombay Presidency Youth Congress over which he presided: Calling for 'the reconstruction of society on another basis', he urged, 'that basis must be one of cooperation, and that is another name for socialism. Our national ideal must, therefore, be the establishment of a cooperative socialist commonwealth'.

1936 is what Rudrangshu Mukherjee describes as 'Jawaharlal's red-vintage year'. In his Presidential Address, much to the annoyance of Gandhiji and the senior members of the Congress Working Committee (whom Bose witheringly dismissed as the 'old guard'), Nehru announced that socialism was not just an economic doctrine but 'a philosophy of life, a vital creed that he held with all his heart'.[13]

Nehruvian socialism desperately needs to be given a fresh lease of life. The Congress has said nothing about it for the last twenty-five years, the very word having been abolished from our vocabulary. It needs to be revived to give the Congress an anchoring in a well-tried ideology that has long served us well. Nehru's socialism was influenced by Marxism but was not an imported thought. Arising from India's social

[13] *Ibid.*, p.143.

and economic conditions, it was a practical response to social reality, not a blind dogma. The longer version of the word was the 'socialist pattern of society' but Nehru often used the short-hand word, 'socialism'.

In Nehru's conception, the expression 'socialist pattern of society' comprised a hard political shell—democracy—within which was preserved a soft economic kernel—socialism. I call it the hard outer shell for on full-scope democracy there was no room for compromise. But when it came to the kernel, right from the start there was no fixed ratio between the public and private sectors. In 1955, when the expression 'socialist pattern of society' came into general use, agriculture, overwhelmingly the main segment of the economy, was left entirely in the private sector: there was no collectivization as in the Soviet Union. Even in industry and services, the private sector was largely left to its own devices. Only the railways, the airlines and the Imperial Bank (which later became the State Bank of India) were nationalized. The only other nationalizations were of British firms leaving behind the departing Imperial flag. Where the public sector came into its own was in pioneering new avenues of growth in areas where the private sector either did not have the financial resources to invest and sit out the gestation period, or lacked the will to go into backward areas, or did not have the technological aptitude to enter into uncharted territory. The consequence of the heyday of the public sector was that whereas, at Independence, over ninety percent of India's machinery requirements, even simple hand-tools, were imported, by 1974 that percentage was brought down to nine percent.

Planning, the key instrument for establishing the 'socialist pattern of society' raised the GDP growth rate from the pre-Independence (1914-47) annual average of 0.72 percent to over 3.5 percent—an increase of five times, which, if maintained subsequently, should have led to our economy growing at 15 percent per annum and not the miserable annual average of 5 to 6 percent attained in the years of liberalization. Of course, such massive change in the profile of the economy required course changes in economic policy. The tragedy was that the course changes were portrayed as the consequence of the problems of failure when, in fact, they were occasioned by the problems of success. The disproportionate benefits conferred on the rich has given us a kind of industrial feudalism and led to the distortions and dissatisfaction that characterize the present domestic economic order. Planning too has been abandoned. A return to the Nehruvian vision would restore the balance in favour of inclusive growth, combining accelerated GDP growth rates with 'power to the people' through fully empowered panchayats. This would facilitate an unflinching focus on equity and social justice.

Non-alignment

Jawaharlal Nehru described the foreign policy he formulated for independent India as embarking on an 'uncharted course'.[14] When today we reckon that there

[14]The phrase was used by historian Mridula Mukherjee, Professor of History at Jawaharlal Nehru University, in conversation with the author.

are just under two hundred member-states of the United Nations (UN), whereas at the time of the adoption of the United Nations Charter in 1945 the number of founder-members (which included British India) was only fifty-one, one glimpses just how uncharted was the way forward for close to three-fourths of the nations of the world emerging into liberation of one form or another. Amongst the first to place itself in this comity of nations was India.

The fundamental contradiction India faced was between the world order envisaged in the Charter, which India has consistently championed, and the world order as it actually evolved in the aftermath of the Second World War.

First was the onset of the Cold War, which overthrew the basic assumption that the states constituting the UN were, in fact, united in peace as they had been united in war.[15]

Second was the meretricious demonstration of nuclear weapons as the ultimate weapon of domination, deployed, many believe and believed, less to bring a recalcitrant Japan to its knees than to signpost the pecking order in the post-War world.

Third was the explosion in the wings waiting to happen of close to a hundred and fifty new member-states entering the UN as the sun began setting on

---

[15] '...the very process of marshalling the world into two hostile camps precipitates the conflict which it sought to avoid': Jawaharlal Nehru at Columbia University, 1949. The text of the whole speech may be accessed in *Jawaharlal Nehru: Speeches, 1949-1953*, Publications Division, Ministry of Information and Broadcasting, New Delhi.

empires that for the past several centuries had believed themselves to be invincible.

Fourth was the emergence, along with decolonization, of the imperative of adjusting relatively poor but manpower-and natural-resource-rich nations into a more equitable world economic order.

As fifty of the original fifty-one founder-members of the UN quickly fell into one or the other camp of the Cold War antagonists, it fell to India at Independence to decide with whom to throw in its lot. That was the commencement of the voyage on uncharted seas. The Indian decision to join neither camp was widely seen as eccentricity or opportunism, catering neither to principle nor to national interest.

In attempting to analyse the reasons for this decision to go it alone, one begins, I think, to discover the rationale for the elaboration of foreign policy under the first prime minister (and foreign minister) of independent India, Jawaharlal Nehru.

Independent India's foreign policy grew out of India's struggle for freedom, a struggle unique in the annals of liberation movements in that it was essentially based in a philosophy and practice of non-violence, an ethical principle of long standing that had been successfully translated by Mahatma Gandhi into a political movement of what he called 'passive resistance' to, and 'non-cooperation' with, a governing authority that was infinitely stronger than the people in conventional military, political and economic terms.[16]

---

[16]'A civil resister never seeks to embarrass Government…He attains the goal by creating goodwill, believing as he does that unfailing exercise of goodwill even in the face of unjust acts of a Government can only

It was, in other words, an asymmetrical response to an asymmetrical balance of power. Had the Freedom Movement resorted to armed struggle or guerilla warfare it would have amounted to taking on the Empire on its own terms. But the Mahatma and his followers consistently rejected not only the means employed to keep India in subjugation but also the goals that the Empire took for granted. Moreover, there was an obsession with ends and means that lent an unusual moral imperative to the political struggle.[17] Since such an asymmetrical response shook the Empire at its roots and contributed substantively to the End of Empire, it was inevitable that a foreign policy that grew out of the freedom struggle would also be essentially asymmetrical and infused with a moral purpose.

---

result in goodwill being ultimately returned by the Government', *Young India*, Wednesday, 23 July 1919, cited in *Journey of a Nation*, Academic Foundation, New Delhi, 2011, p.59.

Also, 'Non-violence implies voluntary submission to the penalty for non-cooperation with evil. I am here, therefore, to invite and cheerfully submit to the highest penalty that can be inflicted upon me for what in law is a deliberate crime, and what appears to me to be the highest duty of a citizen': Mahatma Gandhi at his trial in 1922, cited in Arthur Herman, *Gandhi and Churchill*, Hutchinson, UK, 2008, p.359.

[17]See, for example, Jawaharlal Nehru, 'The spiritualization of politics, using the word not in its narrow religious sense, seemed to me a fine idea. A worthy end should have worthy means leading up to it. That seemed not only a good ethical doctrine but sound, practical politics, for the means that are not good often defeat the end in view and raise new problems and difficulties.' *An Autobiography*, Bodley Head, Oxford, 1936, p.73.

Also see Sunil Khilnani's 34th Jawaharlal Nehru Memorial Lecture, 13 November 2002, *Nehru's Faith*, available from jnmfsch@ndb.vsnl.net.in

Therefore, Nehru's India decided on the asymmetrical course of opting out of the quest for dominance[18] which had hitherto characterized international relations since the dawn of history—and, as far as is known, ever since the struggle for survival began on Planet Earth.

Contemporaneously, the struggle for survival, the survival of the fittest and the quest for dominance were evidenced in the division of the world into two rival blocs, one armed with the unprecedented capacity to inflict nightmare punishment on the other in the event of war and soon to be deterred by the other to match destructive capacity with destructive capacity until eventually the two blocs acquired the capacity to destroy everything and everyone fifty-one times over—fifty-one times, presumably, because superpowers apparently felt, like Jacqueline Susann, that Once was Not Enough!

That such should have been the race for power in the half-century following the bloodletting of two world wars that had rendered the first half of the twentieth century the bloodiest in history, destroying close to fifty million living human beings, was not a race to which a nation liberated through non-violence, and brought up on the ethic that the ends do not

---

[18]The phrase is Prime Minister Rajiv Gandhi's. I first heard him use it at an interaction with university students at Mysore on 17 August 1989. Subsequently, he reverted to it in his Address to the Ninth Non-aligned Summit at Belgrade, see *Selected Speeches and Writings*, 1989, Vol. V, Publications Division, New Delhi, p.277, and once again invoked it in his Jawaharlal Nehru Centenary Memorial Lecture, see *Jawaharlal Nehru Memorial Lectures, 1982-1997*, Vol.II, Bhavan's Book University, Mumbai, 1998, p.155.

justify the means, was going to acquiesce to. And it was certainly not going to do so under as proud and self-assured a leader as Jawaharlal Nehru, adored by an overwhelming majority of his people and armed with their democratically-granted assent.

Such an India was not content to merely be non-partisan in the Cold War. It also had something different to tell the world. And it was precisely because India had something to say which no one else was saying that the world paused to listen. Thus, an asymmetrical foreign policy gave an asymmetric influence hugely disproportionate to the material strength of an India which, in conventional terms, would have been paid little heed to if it were merely parroting the words and postures of others.

Non-alignment was a word devised to meet the then extant reality of the world being divided dangerously into two bitterly opposed rival blocs. Nehru ensured that India was the first emerging country—and, at the time, the only one—to resist the blandishments and worse of both blocs to carve an independent path that reflected to the world at large the sovereignty that India had won back from colonial enslavement. He had no intention of making it a movement, but pressure from scores of newly liberated countries, later numbering over a hundred, led to the launching of the Movement of Non-aligned Countries. The end of the Cold War has rendered the term 'non-alignment' somewhat obsolete (although recent developments centred on the Ukraine threaten to take the world back to the brink) but the philosophy behind that expression remains unaltered.

Non-alignment in an unaligned world simply means independence and sovereignty in foreign policy.

In India's case, that freedom of thought and action in foreign policy is circumscribed by our quarrels with Pakistan and China. That opens the wedge to interference in our affairs by outside powers, especially by those who have taken out a contract for themselves to be the arbiter of other people's destinies. For us to become truly independent, the Nehruvian imperative in the twenty-first century is to compose these quarrels through uninterrupted and uninterruptible dialogue so that our neighbourhood becomes truly peaceful and cooperative and based on Nehru's Five Principles of Panchsheel.[19]

---

[19]The Five Principles of Peaceful Coexistence, known in India as the Panchsheel Treaty, are a set of principles to govern relations between states. Their first formal codification in treaty form was in an agreement between China and India in 1954. This agreement stated the five principles as: Mutual respect for each other's territorial integrity and sovereignty; mutual non-aggression; mutual non-interference in each other's internal affairs; equality and cooperation for mutual benefit, and peaceful coexistence.

Why Nehru Matters More Than Ever

Neera Chandhoke

An otherwise ordinary 'first' speech given by India's fourteenth president, Ram Nath Kovind, would have gone unremarked, except for one notable omission. The name of Pandit Jawaharlal Nehru, arguably the foremost leader of the freedom struggle, and India's first prime minister, was spectacularly missing from the inventory of prominent Indians listed by the President. Though the government under Prime Minister Narendra Modi has gone to extraordinary lengths to eliminate references to the architect of democratic India, we expect the head of state to stand above partisan party politics. There is cause for disappointment.

A few days after Mr Kovind's speech, the Bharatiya Janata Party (BJP) published a largish booklet to celebrate the birth centenary of Deen Dayal Upadhyaya. In the section on great leaders of India, 'Mahapurush', the names of Nehru as well as Mahatma Gandhi are conspicuous by their absence. Almost ten lakh senior school students in Uttar Pradesh are forced to study the booklet, appear for an exam, and be rewarded if they perform well. Many of the 'great men' listed in the booklet have never taken part in the freedom struggle, and never been jailed for combating colonialism, unlike Nehru and the Mahatma. But their names occupy pride of place in oral and written histories authored by the BJP. Leaders who fought for independence are simply written off.

The belittling of Pandit Nehru is odd, because the standing of the current prime minister is not validated by writing out a previous prime minister from the annals of history. The future will judge both leaders on their own merit, their success or their failure in managing a complex and plural society, their credentials as democrats, and their political, economic and strategic visions. Both have a place in modern India. What that place is will be decided by history. The current dispensation should take the art of history-writing seriously and not reduce it to pamphleteering. History is important for collective self-understanding, because it enables us to understand where we have come from, and how we got from 'there' to 'here'. Without competent histories that allow us to understand our collective past and present, and help us generate visions for the future, entire generations will lose their bearings.

What the philosopher Jürgen Habermas calls the 'public use of history' should be, for this reason, subjected to strong evaluations. Since the craft has a bearing on the human condition, we ought to distinguish between histories that inspire a democratic, critical sensibility to contain and challenge authoritarianism, from those that feed appetites for absolute power. History, of course, must narrate tales of tyrants and despots, so that we take care not to repeat the errors of the past. But it must also chronicle tales of the triumph of the human spirit, and inspire us to struggle against totalitarianism and suppression of individual freedom.

For the ruling class, history should be important, because it reminds them that absolute power, often won at the expense of human freedom, does not endure. Unexpected moments arise in the life of a society when its members clamour for change, when existing gods are brought down, and new ones erected in their place, condemned to wait for their own downfall. All of us should be wary of changing tides of fortune.

Fortune, wrote the sixteenth century political theorist of Florence, Niccolò Machiavelli, is unpredictable and inexplicable. She is an active sharer in man's making of history, she produces the unforeseen, and she will never be dominated, but will dominate men. That is why Machiavelli advised the Prince of Florence to study history. The public role of history is to remind rulers that fortune is fickle. After all, Nehru, who once led India to freedom, is vilified in his own country by the benighted cyberspace industry. This is short-sighted, because to unremember the man is to forget that there is an alternative to narrow and energy-consuming nationalism.

Despite all attempts, Nehru continues to be remembered by many for his contribution to the institutionalization of democracy, establishing institutions of excellence, and his conviction that poverty and inequality in India cannot be tackled by the market. There is, however, more to a good society: solidarity with struggling people within and outside the country.

Nehru, as one of the most distinguished leaders of Third World solidarity, reached out to the rest of the colonized world, and forged a joint front against colonialism and a reinvented imperialism. He was, by temperament and experience, a cosmopolitan. His frequent visits to Europe, his deep familiarity with the past, and his understanding of the contemporary ideologies of the day, from liberalism to Fabian socialism, to communist internationalism, had convinced him that the future of India was incomplete without the liberation of other colonies.

Nehru's commitment to the independence of the Third World had been shaped by intellectual journeys through history, as well as participation in a number of international conferences such as the Congress of Oppressed Nationalities in Brussels in 1927. He played a prominent role in the 1955 Bandung Conference, which set the stage for the emergence of a new bloc, and a new ideology in global affairs. Representatives of twenty-nine countries from the global South, comprising well over a billion people, met to consider and debate on how they could help each other to neutralize the harmful effects of colonialism, and bring economic and social well-being to their people. Towering over leaders who had won their political spurs by piloting their countries to independence were Nehru, Kwame Nkrumah, the Prime Minister of Ghana, Gamal Abdel Nasser, the President of Egypt, Chou en-Lai, the Premier of China, and Ho Chi Minh, the Prime Minister of Vietnam. The agenda included every topic over which the colonized and the newly decolonized world had agonized for decades—religion, colonialism, sovereignty, and world peace. The Bandung meeting sparked off reflections on the distinct attractions of non-alignment, and of the strengths that a movement of the non-aligned could acquire in global forums.

Interestingly, if one strand of anti-colonial nationalism focused on the idea and the imaginaries of the nation, the second moved away from processes of closed identity formation towards other ways of being in the world. Nehru's cosmopolitanism acknowledged that our political identities are forged in and through conversations not only with people who are like us, but people who belong to other cultures, other countries, other societies and other traditions, but who are like us in many ways.

Contemporary history has not treated this statesman kindly. This is a great pity because today's generation might know what globalization is, but not what cosmopolitanism is about. Even as our society globalizes at a frenetic pace, it has turned inwards and become claustrophobic. History must remember Nehru, he taught us to look outwards, to express solidarity, and to become, in the process, cosmopolitans. We must remember him because we have lost out on something that is rather important: teaching our children that our imaginations and our energies should be harnessed to the cause of the oppressed over the world, that closed-in societies lead to stagnation if not to certain death, and that such societies circumscribe imaginings and truncate visions. We have, perhaps, become lesser human beings.

Preserving the Ancient Palimpsest

Purushottam Agrawal

In the seventy-fifth year of Independence, the Hindutva project of turning India into an authoritarian monocultural state is nearer success than at any other moment in our history. Such a state requires subjects, not thinking citizens (therefore, an iconic road in the heart of the country's capital must be renamed as 'Kartavyapath', or the Road of Duty, and not 'Adhikarpath', the Road of Rights). Crores of us appear to have willingly traded our citizenship for subjecthood, but many crores have not. The spirit of democracy is certainly weaker today, but it has not been extinguished, and it will not be extinguished until the vision of India imagined and shaped by the leading lights of our national movement has not been entirely erased. Of these leaders, Jawaharlal Nehru, as India's first prime minister, did the most to embed the idea of a diverse, democratic and 'enlightened' India in the national consciousness. Sometimes he faltered, falling below his own standards of political conduct, yet it is not an exaggeration to describe him as the 'Maker' of the modern Indian Republic. His place in history is assured, no matter how radically our history is rewritten or obscured by propaganda.

The Parivar and the present Bharatiya Janata Party (BJP) want to create a control state in the name of what it calls 'authentic' Indian tradition or Hindu tradition. But the legacy of Nehru comes in the way—with his modern sensibility, uncompromising and yet rooted in the multivocality of the Indian cultural experience; he could connect with people, he could function as a very effective and beloved 'guru of the nation' and orient the Indian people towards the enlightenment values of democracy and secularism. These are values antithetical to the agenda of communal supremacists and autocrats. It is for this reason that the *Hindutva-vadis* will continue to both despise and fear Nehru. It is for this reason that attempts have been made for decades, and particularly since 2014, to dismantle and destroy his legacy.

*

Celebrations of the 75th Independence Day of India were marked by further intensification of attempts to denigrate Nehru. The ruling party and its troll army did this without pause, which no longer surprises anyone. But sections of the pliant electronic media also chipped in.

Nehru, they reminded us, took the oath of allegiance to the Queen of England while being sworn in as the PM of the interim government of India in September

1946. As if the rest of the interim cabinet, including Sardar Patel and Rajendra Prasad, both claimed by the Sangh Parivar as their own, took some other oath.

Nehru accepted Partition, we were told, and hence did not deserve any respect. We were not told that Vinayak Damodar Savarkar, 'the father of Hindutva', wholeheartedly agreed with Jinnah on the 'two nation theory'; or that Babasaheb Ambedkar not only accepted Partition but also advocated transfer of populations; or that the Communists justified Partition as 'self-determination'. By the mid-1940s, Jinnah in cahoots with elements of the Imperial establishment had succeeded in creating a situation where Partition was inevitable, a fact recognized with sadness by both Nehru and Patel.

Another favourite theme of right-wing Nehru baiters is that he was solely responsible for the Kashmir imbroglio; had things been left to Patel, everything would have been fine. Patel, however, was rather inclined to give away Kashmir, provided Pakistan stopped supporting the antics of the Hyderabad Nizam. Moreover, Syama Prasad Mukherjee, founder of the Bharatiya Jan Sangh, the predecessor of the BJP, was a minster in the Nehru cabinet which took all the decisions vis-à-vis Kashmir.

But why bother with facts and reason in this post-Truth era?

No low is low enough for the hate Nehru project; his family life, his eating habits, his friends, even personal tragedies—everything is fair game. In late 2017, the head of the BJP's IT cell, Amit Malviya, tweeted a collage of pictures of Jawaharlal Nehru with different women in order to portray him as a philanderer. In three of the nine pictures, Nehru is hugging his sister Vijaya Lakshmi Pandit and being kissed on the cheek by his niece Nayantara. In a fourth, he's congratulating a family friend, Mrinalini Sarabhai, after her classical dance performance. In the rest, he is receiving or seeing off public figures and official guests like Jackie Kennedy and the Mountbattens' young daughter Pamela.

Lies and misinformation assume respectable scholarly forms as well. Over the last couple of years, a number of 'academic' studies have appeared, using facts selectively, distorting them or disregarding them altogether in order to show Nehru in a bad light. In 2021, a major publishing house released a book on India-China relations—*The Long Game: How the Chinese Negotiate with India*—by a top civil servant, recently retired, Vijay Gokhale. In it, he informs his readers nonchalantly, 'Despite the mutual bitterness and recrimination over the PLA [China's People's Liberation Army] invasion at the end of 1950, Mao Zedong himself was the chief guest at India's first Republic Day celebrations in January 1951.'[1] I was flabbergasted: this came from a former foreign secretary of India who had also been our ambassador to China and head of the China and East Asia desk in the Ministry of Eternal Affairs. As is common knowledge, Mao never visited any foreign country except the Soviet Union; and a basic fact check should have revealed to the author and publisher that the chief guest at India's first republic day celebration—in

[1]Vijay Gokhale, *The Long Game: How The Chinese Negotiate with India*, Penguin, Gurugram, 2021, p.31.

1950, incidentally—was President Sukarno of Indonesia, and on 26 January 1951—our *second* Republic Day—it was King Tribhuvan of Nepal. But again, why bother even with rudimentary facts when the idea is to show that Nehru went to any extent to please the Chinese and was therefore responsible for the 1962 defeat?

How different is this kind of scholarship from the WhatsApp and YouTube versions of history with which the right-wing trolls flood the internet and social media? The success of this campaign of ingratitude, besides reflecting the decay in the moral health of society, is also detrimental to the future of our nation. Nehru is not merely history, he continues to be a contemporary challenge to the politics inspired by 'that strange philosophy' which Nehru had recognized as dangerous back in 1933—a philosophy which, besides propagating German-Aryan superiority and 'culling' of 'inferior' races, also held that 'the age of pure reason and unprejudiced science is over'.[2]

Political Hindutva is a poorly Hinduized version of this 'strange philosophy'—which rejects the universal human values represented by modernity and enlightenment, but embraces the amoral techno-bureaucratic aspects of modernity. The ideal state in this philosophy is a control-freak state and the ideal citizen submits to prejudices, hatred and fear instead of conducting life in the light of sensitivity and rational judgement. That is why demagoguery, a belligerent communalized nationalism and the bogey of hurt

[2]*Glimpses of World History*, Penguin, Gurugram, 2004, p. 1065.

sentiments are so crucial to political systems built upon religious fundamentalism and a fixed, 'authentic' cultural identity, of which Hindutva politics is a copybook example.

The 2014 election verdict, which gave the BJP a full majority on its own, was an important stage in the journey towards 'the Hinduization of all politics', to quote the 'father of Hindutva'. For Savarkar, 'Hindutva is *not* identical' to 'that vague, more limited, sectarian term Hinduism'. What Savarkar desired and what the RSS and the entire Sangh-parivar has been attempting for decades is not to make people more religious or more nationalistic, but to make them *Hindu nationalists*. Their true cause has been neither Hinduism nor nationalism, but Hindutva—and their aim is to use the state apparatus to consolidate the Hindutva idea of India, which is necessarily opposed to a democratic Indian nationalism. This is where Nehru becomes a problem: his idea of 'Bharat Mata' is a powerful challenge to the idea of 'Bharat Mata' that the Sangh-parivar has used to try and claim India for itself, and itself alone.

Our freedom movement was unique in the sense that it harnessed patriotic feelings and anti-colonial sentiment to build a democratic, inclusive nationalism. It was described by the remarkable freedom fighter and social reformer Dada Dharmadhikari as '*Manavnishtha Bharatiyata*', or humane Indian nationalism.[3] Reactionary, communal forces of all hues have always been opposed

[3]*Manavnishtha Bharatiyata*, Sarv Sewa Sangh, Varanasi, 2000. First published in 1948.

to this version of nationalism, and that is why Nehru and other leaders of our independence movement counterposed their nationalism to communalism—Hindu, Muslim or any other. Instead of shying away from nationalism, they tried to bring people on board to the idea of *Manavnishtha Bharatiyata* as a shared vision, and they were successful.

The Indian freedom movement, ever mindful of the specificity of the Indian tradition, attempted to make it richer by weaving modern European ideas and institutions into public life. Listening to any of the major voices of those days—political, literary, philosophical or artistic—one can see how nuanced and progressive these attempts were. They 'discovered' the tools to forge a confident, humane and inclusive nationalism that could oppose colonial rule and claim India for every Indian. They discovered these tools in three major civilizations at that historical moment—Indic, West Asian and the European. Instead of lamenting the loss of 'purity' (which in fact is a terminal disease for any culture), and avoiding the pitfalls of extremes, they celebrated the diversity of their cultural experience and intellectual resources.

It is true that a 'dissociation of sensibility' was inevitable among the educated elite and literati of the time, as in any colonized society—a certain alienation from their own society, a distance from their own people. Some glorified this as true modernity, to counter those who claimed that all glory and all modern achievements belonged in India's mythical past. Both these approaches were of course two sides of the same coin of cultural diffidence and a subconscious sense of inferiority.[4] But the finest leaders of our freedom movement were both self-aware and sensitive, and they tried to overcome the dissociation and diffidence. Each one of them launched a personal 'discovery of India'. Gandhi, Tagore, Nehru and Ambedkar, in spite of many sharp differences among themselves, are the most inspiring examples of leaders who engaged in such transformational discoveries. And Nehru's project of discovery was perhaps the most remarkable of all, considering the lifestyle of immense privilege and security that he gave up.

The major figures of our national movement acted as enlighteners appealing to reason and sensitivity, not as entertainers exploiting the baser instincts and sentiments of people. They knew intuitively as well as historically the danger of fascistic transformation of individuals and communities inherent in the politics of fixed cultural and religious identities. But such dangerous transformation was exactly the project of the Hindutva groups, the Hindu Mahasabha and the Rashtriya Swayamsevak Sangh (RSS). It was also the project of Jinnah and his Muslim League. In January 1940 Jinnah had a meeting with Ambedkar and Periyar, in order to forge an alliance that would, ultimately, strengthen the Muslim League's sectarian agenda. Gandhi, sensing the possibility of the emergence of a 'front of Indians opposed to the Congress', requested Jinnah to 'give a

---

[4]For an elaboration see, Purushottam Agrawal, *Kabir, Kabir: The Life and Work of the Early Modern Poet-philosopher*, Chapter III, Westland, New Delhi, 2021.

lead to the Muslims and others' in order to 'free the country from the communal incubus', because sectarian and identitarian politics would undermine the movement for independence.[5] Jinnah dismissed the suggestion. By the 1940s, fighting colonial rule was no longer his priority.

The fight against Imperial rule had, of course, never been a priority for the Mahasabha or the RSS. The Hindutva family as an organized political force hardly made any contribution to the freedom movement. And so, of late, it has been trying to appropriate Gandhi, Patel, Bose, even Bhagat Singh and Ambedkar in order to gain historical legitimacy. But Nehru must be marginalized, denigrated, if not totally erased from the national memory. Why? Because he is a peculiar challenge—take away the constant noise and smoke of vicious propaganda and he will always remain relatable for both the aspirational and the traditional Indian: if he could quote from the popular texts of Hinduism, Buddhism, Islam and Christianity, he could also champion science and technology and call dams and factories the 'temples of India' (and no one's sentiments were hurt).

Nehru was the most consistently modern of our national leaders, but (to the great chagrin of Hindutva) his idea of modernity never implied a violent break from or contempt for tradition. He was most forthright in recognizing his 'dissociation of sensibility' and tried

---

[5]Ishtiaq Ahmed, *Jinnah: His Successes, Failures and Role in History*, Penguin, Gurugram, 2020, p.201.

sincerely to overcome it. Even before coming in close contact with Gandhi, Nehru had made two significant discoveries. One, the distance between those like himself, 'nurtured in an atmosphere of the west', and 'the masses'. Writing about the farmers' agitation in Awadh in January 1921, he remarked, 'It is not the masses but we, nurtured in an atmosphere of the west, who talk glibly of the inefficiency of peaceful methods. The masses know the power of Ahimsa.'[6] The second significant discovery he made was the crucial difference between formal education and instinctive wisdom. He wrote: 'The old epics of India, the *Ramayana* and the *Mahabharata* and other books...were widely known among the masses, and every incident and story and moral in them was engraved on the popular mind and gave a richness and content to it. Illiterate villagers would know hundreds of verses by heart and their conversation would be full of references to them or to some story with a moral enshrined in some old classic. Often, *I was surprised by some such literary turn given by a group of villagers to a simple talk about present day affairs*'[7] (emphasis added).

Nehru's dialogue with tradition became deeper after developing a nuanced relationship with Gandhi. Contrary to popular opinion, Gandhi was not a 'traditionalist' pure and simple; he looked at tradition through the prism of the sensibility of vernacular bhakti poets, who articulated

[6]S. Gopal, ed., *Selected Works of Jawaharlal Nehru*, Orient Longman, New Delhi, 1972, Vol. 1, p.211.

[7]*The Discovery of India*, Gurgaon, 2010, p.61.

India's own early modernity. Gandhi discovered the Gujarati bhakti poet Narsi Mehta—whose song 'Vaishnav Jan to tene kahiye' became his signature tune—before he came to the Bhagvad Gita (which, incidentally, he read first in English translation). The Gandhi-Nehru dialogue, thus, was between the vernacular modernity emerging from within Indian tradition and the Western version of modernity. It went a long way in making Nehru the thoroughly *Indian* modern mind that he became.

Andre Malraux, the French intellectual, described Nehru as 'the nation's guru, just as Gandhi had been'.[8] Dipesh Chakrabarty places Nehru in the 'crop of leaders' produced by decolonization 'who saw themselves fundamentally as teachers to their nations'.[9] A good teacher learns from the 'taught' as well. Nehru's learning led to the firm belief that individual human beings are not mere ciphers of their cultural tradition and identity, and must be treated as autonomous moral agents capable of making their own choices: 'I do not idealize the conception of masses and as far as possible, I try to avoid thinking of them as a theoretical abstraction... I try to think of them as individuals rather than as vague groups.'[10] His insistence that 'the country must conduct itself through political principles, not through religious sentiments' was the natural outcome of this belief, which did not imply any insensitivity to religious traditions or faith.

---

[8] *Anti-Memoirs*, Penguin, London, 1968, p.164.

[9] *The Crises of Civilization*, Oxford University Press, 2018, p.46.

[10] *The Discovery of India*, p.50.

Nehru's idea of India comes out poignantly in his choice of metaphor for its cultural continuity and 'unity in diversity'. The better-known metaphor for this is Tagore's: the great ocean of humanity. But the ocean devours the individuality of the rivers joining it. Nehru, mindful of the individuality of all the contributors to national life, sees India differently: 'She was like an ancient palimpsest on which layer upon layer of thought and reverie had been inscribed, and yet no succeeding layer had completely hidden or erased what had been written previously. All of these existed in our conscious or subconscious selves, though we may not have been aware of them, and they had gone to build up the complex and mysterious personality of India.'[11] Nehru also notes, that 'those who professed a religion of non-Indian origin, or coming down to India settled down there, became distinctively Indian in the course of a few generations'.[12]

The palimpsest metaphor authentically represents the cultural history of India, and the dynamics of 'conscious or subconscious selves' of *all* Indians.

Hindutva forces have been quite aware of the power of Nehru's magic, which consists of discarding the lure of extremes in favour of the enlightened middle path, where multiple Indias can live in relative harmony. To counter this, they try to project him as 'anti-Hindu'—for example, by attributing a description of Nehru by a Hindu Mahasabha leader—'Englishman by education,

[11]*Ibid.*, p.55.

[12]*Ibid.*, p.51.

Muslim by culture, Hindu merely by accident'—to Nehru himself! (A comprehensive fact-check by Alt News has completely exposed this sleight of hand.[13])

This kind of propaganda, going on for years, failed to make much of a dent in Nehru's popularity among Hindus. The recent success of such projections has a lot to do with the hegemonic status acquired by the post-modern politics of identity, and the propaganda deluge online and in the pro-establishment media since 2014. But many intellectuals and academics whom we would not associate with the Hindu Right have also contributed to this discourse. Perhaps Nehru's connect with 'religious' Indians (given his typically modern, unambiguous aversion to institutionalized religiosity) seems surprising to these liberal commentators and confuses them.

Back in 2004, I was attending a conference of scholars of Indian religions and cultures at Esalen Institute, California and was amazed to hear from a very respected scholar of philosophy and history that 'the rise of Hindutva politics in India is due to the fact that Nehru suppressed religion, particularly its public display'. Any Indian born and brought up in 'Nehru's India' would find this statement bizarre. Nehru and his colleagues were farsighted, and in continuation of Gandhi's idea that 'every religion has some element of Truth', tried to evolve a state which sought to neither privilege nor

---

[13]Arjun Sidharth, 'Did Jawaharlal Nehru ever say "I am English by education, Muslim by culture and Hindu by accident"?', Alt News, 5 November 2018.

suppress any religion or its public display, and provided space to atheists as well. This was in continuity with the Indian way of looking at these matters.

Even more astonishing is Shashi Tharoor's assessment of Nehru's views on religion and spirituality. Tharoor's 2003 book *Nehru: The Invention of India* represents the typical thinking of the successful urban middle class—generally innocent of history and hence very vocally opposed to the so-called 'big government'. The short book is littered with nuggets of neoliberal wisdom such as this: '[Nehru's] foreign policy was an end in itself rather than a means to promote the security and well-being of the country in whose name it was conducted'.[14] I have commented on some of these observations elsewhere;[15] here let us discuss only religion and spirituality. According to Tharoor, Nehru 'created the technological institutions that have positioned India for leadership in the computer age, but he did not understand that software and spirituality could go hand in hand, that India in the twenty-first century would be a land of both programming and prayer'.[16]

Really? This about a man who in a 1960 conversation with R.K. Karanjia emphasized the depressing effects of the 'spiritual emptiness' caused by 'technological civilization' and underlined the responsibility of society

[14]*Nehru: The Invention of India*, Arcade Publishing, New York, 2003, p.184.

[15]See preface to '*Kaun Hain Bharat Mata': Itihas, Sanskriti aur Bharat ki Sankalpna* (Hindi), Rajkamal Prakashan, New Delhi, 2021.

[16]*Nehru: The Invention of India*, pp.250-51.

and the state to address this emptiness?[17] Surely Tharoor had read Nehru's writings before he wrote on the man. How, then, did he miss the poignant ruminations on religion and spirituality not only in Nehru's essays but also in his well-known books, *The Discovery of India* and *An Autobiography*?

But yes, Nehru would hardly have any patience with the 'spirituality' peddled by the likes of 'Sadhguru' and 'Sri Sri'. Like Gandhi and Tagore, he had earned a nuanced understanding of spirituality, and looked at religion historically in conjunction with philosophy and science. In *The Discovery of India*, he confesses his aversion to the 'superstitious practices and dogmatic beliefs' and 'uncritical credulousness' that often go with religion. But he also notes that 'religion had supplied some deeply felt inner need of human nature, and the vast majority of people all over the world could not do without some form of religious belief… It had given a set of values to human life, and though some of these values had no application today, or were even harmful, others were still the foundation of morality and ethics'.[18]

Towards the end of the book, he writes, '[A] small aspect of infinite, eternal truth is apprehended by the human mind in a form limited by the time, space and prevailing ideology; hence it has ever to be so sought, renewed and reshaped.' He then proceeds to analyse ways of discovering the truth:

[17]R.K. Karanjia, *The Mind of Mr Nehru*, George Allen and Unwin, London, 1960, p.25.

[13]*The Discovery of India*, p.13.

> Religion—though it has undoubtedly brought comfort to innumerable human beings and stabilized society by its values—has checked the tendency to change and progress inherent in human society. Philosophy has…encouraged thought and inquiry. But, it has usually lived in its ivory tower…concentrating on ultimate purposes and failing to link them with the life of man… Science ignored ultimate purposes and looked at fact alone. It made the world jump forward with a leap…for the first time it was possible to conceive that man could triumph over and shape his physical environment… [Yet] some vital link was missing. There was no knowledge of ultimate purpose, and not even an understanding of the immediate purpose… Nor did man, so powerful in his control of nature, have the power to control himself and the monster he had created run amok.[19]

Nehru insistently makes a distinction between utilitarian use of technology and developing the 'temper and approach of science', and also reiterates the need for faith:

> Whether we believe in God or not, it is impossible not to believe in something, whether we call it a creative life-giving force or vital energy inherent in matter which gives it its capacity for self-movement and growth, or by some other name,

[19]*Ibid.*, pp.569-70.

> something that is as real, though elusive, as life is real when contrasted with death. Whether we are conscious of it or not most of us worship at the altar of some unknown god...some vital force, urges us on and we tread that path from generation to generation.[20]

And how did he himself relate with this 'creative life giving' force? He states very early in *The Discovery of India*:

> I can appreciate to some extent the conception of monism, and I have been attracted towards the *advaita* (non-dualist) philosophy of the Vedanta... [But the] diversity and fullness of nature stir me and produce a harmony of the spirit, and I can imagine myself feeling at home in the old Indian or Greek pagan and pantheistic atmosphere, but minus the conception of God or gods that was attached to it. Some kind of ethical approach to life has a strong appeal for me, though it would be difficult for me to justify it logically. I have been attracted by Gandhiji's stress on right means and I think one of his greatest contributions to our public life has been this emphasis.[21]

It is only the votaries of political Hindutva and the followers of the peculiar '*Amrikapanthi*' branch of NRI Hinduism who are violently troubled by Nehru's

[20] *Ibid.*, p.572.

[21] *Ibid.*, p.16.

enlightened approach. Otherwise, anyone nurtured within the Indian religious sensibility would immediately relate to what Nehru is saying here. Diversity, tolerance of difference and a variety of ethical approaches to life have been facts of India's social life for centuries.

This sensitive and nuanced engagement with matters of faith and tradition made for an enduring connect with the people who elected Nehru to the office of prime minister with the kind of mandate that leaders dream of. It was a truly popular mandate—from every community, class and region—and Nehru did not have to spend every waking hour in campaign mode to earn this mandate.

Nehru is vilified by the Hindu right because after Independence he had the historic opportunity and responsibility to lead the process of channelling the innate patriotism of his fellow citizens into a modern version of *Manavnishtha Bharatiyata*—an Indian nationalism which was forward-looking yet rooted in our tradition and heritage; which was inclusive and assertive of national interest and pride. And in this he succeeded spectacularly—defying the doom-and-gloom predictions of many pundits within and outside India and, with an overwhelming majority of the Indian people behind him, mounting the greatest challenge to the fascistic cult of 'authenticity', majoritarianism and brute power.

The Hindutva lot may not study Nehru academically, but politically they know very well the seriousness of the challenge he still poses to them, which is why there will be no let-up in the campaign to tarnish his image. There is nothing we can do about the generals and foot-soldiers of Hindutva, but at least the progressives and liberals among us should engage seriously with his views on culture, faith and history instead of passing spurious judgements. They will not be doing any favour to Nehru, only contributing to the ethical task of preserving the ancient palimpsest that is India.

the processes of reasoning, are the greatest resources we have through which to create and sustain our moral imagination.

The conventional understanding of Nehru as indifferent to religion is not untrue. But it is not wholly true either. There were times in his life when he was deeply drawn to religious texts and ideas. One such period was when he was in jail in 1921–22, during the Non-cooperation Movement.

I recently found two remarkable letters written by Nehru to Gandhi in the early months of 1922. These letters do not appear in the *Selected Works of Jawaharlal Nehru,* nor have they been quoted by Nehru biographers. A recent collection of Nehru–Gandhi letters published by the Oxford University Press does not contain them either.

These letters may have been overlooked by scholars because they rest not in the Nehru papers in New Delhi but in the Gandhi papers in Ahmedabad. Yet the letters are important, not least because they complicate the received understanding of Nehru's approach to religion.

Both these letters to Gandhi are handwritten; both were sent from the same address, the District Jail in Agra. The first letter is dated 9 January 1922. Here, Nehru mentions what he has been reading in prison—namely, mostly religious books. Thus he writes: 'I have read Glover's *Jesus of History*—a book of absorbing interest, and have also done a good deal of the Bible in the light thereof. I have begun seriously reading the *Ramayan*—Tulsi too, and Kabir's bhajans and slokas from Bhagavad Gita serve as memory exercises whilst

Nehru the Spiritualist

Ramachandra Guha

In an important essay published some years ago, Sunil Khilnani argued that 'Nehru was a politician without religious faith, but in possession of the deepest moral sense. He tried to develop a morality without the fallback of religion, and while having to act under the compulsions of wielding power'.

That Nehru was sceptical of religion is widely believed. Khilnani begins his essay with a letter written by Nehru to Gandhi in 1933, where he stated: 'Religion is not familiar ground for me, and as I have grown older, I have definitely drifted away from it.' He then quotes from Nehru's autobiography, published in 1936, where Nehru said that 'organized religion' filled him 'with horror...almost always it seemed to stand for a blind belief and reaction, dogma and bigotry, superstition and exploitation'.

In most civilizations and cultures, religion has been seen as a source of morality. Nehru was a moral person, but without basing his values in religion. This is how Khilnani sums up Nehru's faith: 'Reason, and the processes of reasoning, are the greatest resources we have through which to create and sustain our moral imagination.'

The conventional understanding of Nehru as indifferent to religion is not untrue. But it is not wholly true either. There were times in his life when he was deeply drawn to religious texts and ideas. One such period was when he was in jail in 1921-22, during the Non-cooperation Movement.

I recently found two remarkable letters written by Nehru to Gandhi in the early months of 1922. These letters do not appear in the *Selected Works of Jawaharlal Nehru*, nor have they been quoted by Nehru biographers. A recent collection of Nehru-Gandhi letters published by the Oxford University Press does not contain them either.

These letters may have been overlooked by scholars because they rest not in the Nehru papers in New Delhi but in the Gandhi papers in Ahmedabad. Yet the letters are important, not least because they complicate the received understanding of Nehru's approach to religion.

Both these letters to Gandhi are handwritten; both were sent from the same address, the District Jail in Agra. The first letter is dated 9 January 1922. Here, Nehru mentions what he has been reading in prison—namely, mostly religious books. Thus he writes: 'I have read Glover's *Jesus of History*—a book of absorbing interest, and have also done a good deal of the Bible in the light thereof. I have begun seriously reading the *Ramayan*—Tulsi too, and Kabir's bhajans and slokas from Bhagavad Gita serve as memory exercises whilst

I have my morning and evening walks. I have, as you might well imagine, regularly done my prayers, regularly retired at the time appointed by you, and been out of bed at the same hour when, as Nanak says the "Heavens rain nectar".'

Later in the same letter, Nehru remarks: 'My days are passed among the saints nowadays, and I should love to finish as well as I can my knowledge of the Bible, the Saints (including Christian Saints of course), the *Ramayan* and the *Mahabharat* (including of course the Bhagavad Gita). I have some secular literature [with me], no doubt, but that takes frankly, a subordinate place. The memorizing of songs and verses is a grand thing—it puts me in mind of the great times when our men and women lived and moved as men and women and carried the treasures of all their religious and philosophical lore in the impregnable fortresses of their memories.'

The second letter was written four weeks later, on 19 February 1922. Nehru had recently been joined in prison by one 'Khwaja Saheb' from Aligarh. 'It is a privilege to learn Urdu from Khwaja,' writes Nehru to Gandhi. 'It is such a stately script, almost symbolic of the easy splendours of the Mussalman.' Apart from teaching Nehru the Urdu script, Khwaja gave him 'a few couplets from Urdu poets every day, and important verses from the Koran. I in my turn give Khwaja something from the Upanishads and propose to give him something from the Gita'.

Meanwhile, with another fellow prisoner, one Ram Nareshji, Nehru had finished the sections of the

Ramayana named 'Balakand' and 'Ayodhyakand'. 'I hope to finish the rest in about twenty days,' wrote Nehru to Gandhi, 'as I finished "Sundarakand" in Naini [jail] and the rest is plain sailing. It is a joy to read [the] *Ramayan* every morning. When a quiet early hour of the night is selected for reading it, one almost melts in the liquid love of Tulsi. *Ramayan* is more a spiritual autobiography than a poetic history of Rama'.

There is a poetic quality to Nehru's own descriptions too. Clearly, he was loving his time with sacred literature. At this time in his life, secular works were taking a 'subordinate place' to texts written (and sung) at a time when Indian men and women 'carried the treasures of all their religious and philosophical lore'.

When these letters were written, Nehru was in his early thirties. He had lately fallen under the spell of Gandhi, whose own faith was both religious as well as eclectic, drawing from several different sources. The three religious thinkers Gandhi most often invoked were the Vaishnava poet Narsinh Mehta, the Jain philosopher Raychandbhai, and the heterodox Christian Leo Tolstoy. It may have been the Mahatma's influence that made the young Nehru, in jail, soak himself in the texts and traditions of Hinduism, Islam, Christianity and Sikhism.

However, within a decade of writing these letters to Gandhi, Nehru seems to have left behind his enchantment with religion. Why? During the Non-cooperation movement Hindus and Muslims worked shoulder to shoulder. But later in the decade the communities began to drift apart, and there were a series of Hindu-Muslim riots in Northern India. Perhaps

Nehru now believed that religion was a dangerous and divisive force in Indian politics, and had best be kept out of the discussion.

In the 1930s, Nehru also became influenced by Western socialism. This prided itself on its secular, scientific ethos, and was implacably opposed to expressions of religious faith. While in jail in 1921-22 Nehru had little time for secular literature—now, that was all he was reading.

The Partition riots of 1947 furthered Nehru's distaste for organized religion. The malign activities of the Muslim League on the one side and of hardline Hindu groups such as the Rashtriya Swayamsevak Sangh on the other, convinced him that sectarian identities were a danger to the unity of India. As he put it in a letter to his chief ministers in December 1952, the nation must not be allowed to 'go astray in the crooked paths of provincialism, communalism, casteism and all other disruptive and disintegrating tendencies'.

The Nehru of the 1940s and 1950s wished to promote a 'scientific temper' among the Indian masses. Religion, he felt, had absolutely no place in the process of nation-building. India must never become a 'Hindu Pakistan'.

However, as he grew older, Nehru began to see that while it must be kept far away from politics, religious faith could still play a role in an individual's quest for truth and tranquillity. In his last years, Nehru often visited my home town, Dehradun. He came partly because he loved the views of the Himalayas and partly to spend time with a spiritual teacher who lived on the road between Dehradun and Rajpur. Her name was Anandmayi Ma. A Bengali Hindu by birth, her faith (like Gandhi's) was ecumenical—she interacted with Muslims, Christians and Parsis as well as Hindus.

Nehru's visits to Anandmayi Ma were kept hidden from the public. But they were spoken about in the Dehradun of my boyhood. Much later, the historian and biographer B.R. Nanda, who knew Nehru well, confirmed to me that towards the end of his life the prime minister had regular interactions with Anandmayi Ma. In his youth, Nehru spent some of his time reading about the saints; in his old age, conversing with one of them.

It is notable, however, that Nehru sought out not an accredited head of a famous Hindu temple but a mystic who lived in seclusion. He had no time for Sankaracharyas, but he did, at least in his last days, have much time for Anandmayi Ma, who—like his long dead mentor, Gandhi—did not believe that any single religion or religious text had a privileged pathway to God.

What the two spoke about in Dehradun is alas not known. But that they met, and quite often, further complicates our understanding of Nehru's faith. He was clearly not always the aggressive atheist some of his admirers, and many of his detractors, have made him out to be. In his twenties and thirties, Nehru was deeply moved by the Gita, by Tulsi's *Ramayana*, and by some Christian texts as well. In his forties and fifties, when he was at the apex of his own career, Nehru believed that by rationality alone would man understand (if not conquer) the world. Still later, in his seventies, with his health fading and the end visibly near, he turned once more to the consolations of religion.

The Platonic Republican: Philosopher-Statesman

Kumar Ketkar

If indeed Jawaharlal Nehru had been assassinated, as some RSS (Rashtriya Swayamsevak Sangh) activists desired and have said so publicly in recent times,[1] how would the history of post-Independence India have been shaped? It is not as though we have heard that bizarre thought for the first time. Books have been written, police and inquiry commissions' reports have been published and the court proceedings of the Mahatma Gandhi murder trial are available. There are also press interviews of Gopal Godse (brother of Nathuram Godse and a co-conspirator in Gandhiji's assassination on 30 January 1948) and others. All those documents reveal that the conspiracy was to kill most of the top leadership of the Congress. The 'crime' of the Congress leaders was, argued the murderers, that they were responsible for the partition of India.

---

[1]Ref. article by BJP member B. Gopalkrishnan in *Kesari*, Malayalam edition, Kerala, 17 October 2014.

Apparently, there was no such aggrieved feeling or moral outrage against Muhammad Ali Jinnah. So the assassins and their masters did not conspire to kill the leader of the Pakistan movement. The Hindutva fanatics, it seems, did not hold Jinnah responsible for the 'crime'. Partition, according to them, was the sin only of the Congress leaders. Gandhiji and Nehru, of course, were their prime targets. But we must remember that it is a cunning political tactic of the Sangh Parivar to say that the assassination was a spontaneous and patriotic outburst, thus implying that neither the RSS nor the Hindu Mahasabha (HMS) were even remotely involved!

What is not disclosed or discussed is the fact that the attempts on Gandhiji's life had begun as early as 1933. Thanks to Teesta Setalvad's researched compilation of all the relevant documents, *Beyond Doubt: A Dossier on Gandhi's Assassination*,[2] we are reminded of the conspiracies that were being hatched years before the plans for Partition became an agenda. It is obvious, therefore, that hatred for Gandhiji was being drummed up by the fanatic Hindu brigade much before Pandit Nehru emerged as a leader in his own right. So the reasons to plot against Gandhi and Nehru are not the same, nor did they originate at the same time. Nehru was considered a target only after Partition. The tragic fact that Gandhiji was actually killed within six months of Independence adds hypothetical horror to the sinister campaign against Nehru.

The followers of the RSS or Hindu Mahasabha

[2]Pub. Tulika Books, New Delhi, 2015.

did not, however, equate Gandhiji and Nehru. They hated the Mahatma because he was their direct enemy. Gandhiji used to say that he was a proud Hindu. He endorsed Chaturvarnya. Gandhi's idea of Hind Swaraj did not fundamentally challenge the idea of Ram Rajya or the so-called Hindu ethos. Gandhiji was a strict vegetarian and was opposed to cow-slaughter. He advocated abstinence from sex and all material pleasures. He propagated a ban on alcohol. His personal lifestyle was akin to that of an ancient Indian rishi. Many of his followers were 'Acharyas': Acharya Kripalani, Acharya Narendra Dev, Acharya Bhagwat and so on. His centres were known as 'ashrams'. All ashrams observed a strict daily routine and discipline, starting the day with bhajans.

Then what was the issue that made the Hindutva followers hate and despise Gandhiji? The RSS and the HMS had little concern for Hindu philosophy. They were not scholars of the Vedas or the great Indian epics. They were not even clear as to who should be the truly iconic Hindu god. Lord Ram or Lord Krishna? Sita or Draupadi? They could not even decide which 'book' should be the real Holy Book. They had of course shortlisted the Bhagvad Gita. But then, the Gita was studied, taught and discussed in all the Gandhi ashrams too. While Gandhiji and Vinoba Bhave saw in the philosophy of the Gita universal concerns like spirituality and love, the followers of the RSS quoted the Gita to advocate the idea of war and violence to achieve their goal. Gandhiji insisted on the integration of means and ends, the Hindutva brigade believed that the end justified all means.

Be that as it may, the basic difference of approach between Gandhi's philosophy and that of militant Hindutva had little to do with the idea of Hindu philosophy or traditions. The basis of radical Hindutva was being anti-Muslim on communal lines and anti-Islam on political and philosophical lines. Hatred for Muslims and contempt for the so-called 'alien' Islamic culture and religion was the essential content of their discourse. Gandhiji was their direct enemy because he occupied the socio-cultural-political space which they believed was theirs. And Gandhiji's advocacy of '*Ishwar-Allah tera naam*' stood in direct opposition to their idea of Hindu and Muslim communities. The Mahatma's appeal to remove hatred from hearts and minds, and to love all humanity, including Muslims and Christians, was a direct challenge to their social philosophy. To their dismay and disgust, the Congress under Gandhiji had won the people's hearts and had a pan-Indian and international following. There was no chance or possibility to remove Gandhiji from that political space except by way of killing him.

He must be physically eliminated, they thought, because he cannot be fought politically. That is what they did.

★

Jawaharlal Nehru was different. Though he was a follower of Gandhiji, he was less ideological and more political. For Nehru, the Gita was not the guiding light, Karl Marx was. Spirituality was not his credo, science was. Ram Rajya was not his ideal, socialism was. The ashram was not his medium of political congregation, trade unions or Kisan Sabhas were. He was not a vegetarian, nor did he believe that being anti-alcohol was important ideologically. Gandhiji did not believe in the idea of class conflict, Nehru did. Gandhiji never thought of the Russian Revolution as the forward march of history. Nehru wanted to learn from and emulate Lenin. Though both had lived in London, Gandhiji remained quintessentially a traditional Hindu within a Vaishnava ethos. Nehru, on the other hand, represented a dialectical synthesis of the West and the East. Gandhiji advocated freedom from pleasure, Nehru believed in the idea of materialism. Gandhiji thought of sex as almost a sin (notwithstanding his Experiments with Truth), Nehru was against celibacy. Gandhiji looked at large-scale industrialization as destruction of nature and traditional modes of production, Nehru saw in large industry and modern technology the progress of civilization. Both loved nature and thought the preservation of environment a duty, but with different perspectives. Gandhiji looked at tradition as a guide, Nehru thought of modernity as the future and regarded old practices as hurdles to progress.

But all these philosophical or ethical differences cannot be considered inimical in the political sense. In political discourse, there is something known as friendly contradiction vis-à-vis hostile contradiction. That is why the outrageous inference of Markandeya Katju, the former chairman of the Press Council of India and a retired Supreme Court judge, that Gandhiji was a British agent or a right-wing Hindu demagogue, cannot be taken seriously. The differences between Gandhiji and Nehru were known. Even when Jayaprakash Narayan embraced Marxism, he remained Gandhian, just as even when Ram Manohar Lohia advocated socialism, his politics was Gandhian.

Nehru was a follower of Gandhiji and remained so throughout his life. This perplexes and flummoxes many a commentator. But it is not as irrational or hypocritical as it appears to some who highlight their differences to condemn both. Nehru was exactly twenty years younger than Gandhiji. (Mohandas Karamchand was born on 2 October 1869 and Jawaharlal on 14 November 1889.) Both lived in England, Gandhiji during 1881-91 and Nehru during 1905-12. Both were in the capital of the British Empire at the peak of imperialist hegemony. But it was also a period of tremendous intellectual ferment, all over Europe in general and England in particular. The ideas of Karl Marx had begun to take root in the intellectual community of England. The Labour Party was formed in 1900, a couple of years after Karl Marx's works were translated in English. But the ideas of the rights and representation of the working class were already taking shape in England and in Europe even before Marx became an icon. The Liberal Party had begun to espouse the cause of the working classes.

The ideas of nationalism too had begun to influence the émigré students in London. It is interesting to note that Gandhi and Lenin were in London, though not at the same time—Gandhi to study law and Lenin for his political activities. Both were of the same age—Lenin was born on 22 April 1870, just a few months after Gandhi. Vinayak Savarkar, better known as Veer Savarkar and another stalwart of the pro-Independence movement, too studied law in London and was also influenced by the ideas of nationalism in the British capital. Though a staunch Hindu nationalist, to whom the creation of the term Hindutva is attributed, he was deeply impressed by the prevailing ideas of European (specifically Italian!) nationalism. It was not only high-octane political discourse but also heightened intellectual activity that dominated the minds of the youth in London in the late nineteenth and early twentieth centuries.

It was common for the Indian elite to send their children to England to study, the most popular aspiration then being to study law and become a barrister. From Womesh Chandra Banerjee who went to London in 1864 to Romesh Chandra Dutt in 1869; Mohandas Karamchand Gandhi in 1889 to Vallabhbhai Patel in 1911; from Savarkar in 1905 to Dr B.R. Ambedkar in 1922, to Syama Prasad Mukherjee in 1926, the list is long.

Jawaharlal Nehru studied law in London but earlier, at Cambridge, he studied natural sciences and chemistry, botany and geology, and took particular interest in history, economics and literature. The point to note is that the overall influence on all of them was British. In today's parlance, they were the vintage generation of NRIs—the non-resident Indians. But all of them did not imbibe the same ideas or schools of thought. Womesh Chandra Banerjee became the president of the Indian National Congress, Romesh Chandra Dutt became a communist, Savarkar became a militant Hindu nationalist and Ambedkar became the towering leader of the Dalits in India and later the architect of India's Constitution. Gandhiji returned to India and within two years sailed for South Africa and there devised totally new ideas of carrying out political activities. Satyagraha and non-violence became new forms of struggle as well as a new philosophy of life.

Nehru returned to India in 1912, at the age of twenty-three, thrilled by the great scientific ideas of Albert Einstein, the philosophical works of Bertrand Russell and the political thought of socialism. So this vintage generation of NRI intellectuals and activists developed diverse ideas about Indian nationalism. Gandhiji came back to India three years after Nehru. Young Jawaharlal was looking for some radical groups to join, much on the lines of the Fabian socialist and trade union movements in England. He did not find any and was a little disappointed after attending a Congress session dominated by the moderates. He was in a sort of political wilderness, though psychologically he was committed to the ideas of progressive, socialistic nationalism.

Nehru felt that he was vindicated in his socialist beliefs, when, in 1917, the Russian Revolution transformed the landscape of world politics. The Russian Revolution ignited considerable intellectual curiosity, though very little literature was available then. Lokmanya Tilak wrote a series of articles in his paper, *Kesari*, paying tribute to Lenin and the Bolshevik Revolution in Russia. Indeed, Lenin is known to have inquired who this person Tilak was! In the early phase of his political life, Tilak was known as a Hindu revivalist leader of the nationalist movement. But politics was rapidly changing not only in India but internationally, particularly after the Leninist Revolution. Lokmanya Tilak was emerging as a radical leader of the working masses and peasants and not as a Hindu leader. When briefly in England, where he had gone to argue for himself in a case lodged against him, Tilak addressed a Labour Party meeting, with George Bernard Shaw on the same platform.

In the year 1920, the All India Trade Union Congress (AITUC) was formed, on the lines of the Trade Union Congress (TUC) in England and with communist ideological underpinnings. Nehru became associated with it almost immediately and became its president in 1929. It is no coincidence that just two years earlier he had visited the Soviet Union and was impressed by its achievements in the very first decade after the Revolution. It is obvious that Nehru was evolving a parallel political line within the Congress, even as Gandhi had emerged as the supreme leader of the party after 1921.

As Nehru's autobiography reveals, he was quite often frustrated and annoyed by Gandhiji's style and spirituality. His fasts and his food fads, his sudden withdrawal from agitational campaigns and his methods of personal 'purification' for 'sins' like caste discrimination or some violent incident in the movement, often confounded Nehru. But he also saw the massive following that Gandhi had among the poor, the genuineness of his indefinite fasts, the total dedication and philosophical detachment that created a halo around the Mahatma. Nehru wrote that the moment Gandhiji entered the room, the atmosphere became electric and everybody present felt enthusiastic and inspired. Gandhiji's connect and credibility among people was astonishing and unprecedented.

Nehru also realized that the British Empire was so confounded by this 'fakir' that it often succumbed to his mystic charms. Nehru recognized the fantastic strength of the Mahatma, never ever challenged him, notwithstanding their differences, and chose to follow his wisdom and abide his whims. Nehru realized and respected the fact that Gandhiji was providing a paradigm shift to the idea of freedom. It was not just independence from the British, but also from all forms of oppression within. Many critics of Gandhiji grew to become his admirers. Even a communist leader like B.T. Ranadive, a strident critic during the Freedom Movement, later revised his view and said that Gandhiji was a revolutionary, a moral crusader!

Though Gandhiji had mesmerized the masses, by the mid-1930s Nehru had emerged as an independent leader in his own right. He had a huge following among the peasants of Uttar Pradesh, among the industrial proletariat, educated youth and the middle class and also among the British intelligentsia. Those who were confounded by the inexplicable faddism of Gandhiji found in Nehru a rational, modern and cosmopolitan figure who still had roots among the Indian masses. His writings and speeches as well as his handsome and visibly transparent persona inspired men and women alike.

On the fiftieth anniversary of the Congress in 1936, Pandit Nehru fully established his leadership and with it the vision of independent India. The ideas of liberation from landlordism-zamindari and its feudal clutches, the rights of the workers, the notions of social justice and equality, and his emphasis on science and technology and a secular outlook galvanized the masses. The idea of materialism and socialism, of anti-colonialism and anti-imperialism, of internationalism and universal pacifism had arrived. Nehru had synthesized Gandhian ethics with global politics. He was driven by the idea of transforming the world. The Indian masses felt that the new icon for this brave new world was Nehru.

That is why I raised the question at the beginning of this essay: What if Jawaharlal Nehru was indeed killed soon after Independence and Partition as the conspirators were plotting? Gandhiji was their target even before Partition and if they had succeeded, the Freedom Movement would have taken a different course. By the 1930s, Gandhiji's leadership was established so far and wide that there was no one to take the baton from him at that point of time. Nehru was emerging rapidly as a leader in his own right because of his direct contact with the masses, but had not yet reached the stature of the Mahatma. That began to evolve only after the 1936 Faizpur session of the Indian National Congress.

Nehru came on the radar of the Sangh Parivar only after Gandhiji declared that he would be his successor. Nehru's rising popularity had upset the Parivar, but

Gandhiji confronted the succession issue upfront. Responding to the rumours and public commentary about the growing differences between them, he said, 'Somebody suggested that Jawaharlal and I were estranged. This is baseless. Jawaharlal has been resisting me ever since he fell into my net. You cannot divide water by repeatedly striking it with a stick. It is just as difficult to divide us. I have always said that not Rajaji, nor Sardar Vallabhbhai Patel, but Jawaharlal will be my successor. He says whatever is uppermost in his mind, but he always does what I want. When I am gone, he will do what I am doing now. Then he will speak my language too. After all, he was born in this land. Every day he learns some new thing. He fights with me because I am there. Whom will he fight when I am gone? And who will suffer his fighting? Ultimately he will have to speak my language. Even if this does not happen, I would at least die with this faith.'

Quoting this from *The Collected Works of Mahatma Gandhi* (Vol. 75, pp.219-20), Prof Alok Bajpai says, 'It was essentially a political decision of Gandhi to put a fullstop to the various confusions and gossips about "Who After Gandhi". The timing of the decision is also very significant. The Freedom Movement was reaching its highest point in the shape of Quit India. Internal rivalries, political competition, ego clashes and of course differing opinions were coming [out] on the surface. This was not a question of "just political power" but a natural culmination of [a] democratically constituted Indian national movement. Gandhi by this decision tried to settle the issue of his legacy to be carried forward, at least in the political domain.'[3]

Gandhi and Nehru were in complete agreement, however, on the most important and explosive issue of communalism. Gandhiji's critics as well as his Hindu protagonists often quote his assertion that he was a proud Hindu. But they conveniently ignore his position that he was opposed to the concept of organized religion and the religious foundation of nationalism. 'One's own religion is after all a matter of oneself and one's Maker and no one else's,' was his belief. Gandhiji's religion essentially meant public and private morality. That was his politics too. Theism or atheism did not really matter for him in politics or even religion. Gandhiji had also noted with total appreciation Nehru's grasp of international politics and his perspective on world affairs. For Nehru, socialism was an ideology and a modern political-philosophical system. For Gandhiji, however, socialism was nothing but a compassionate and moral approach towards poverty, sorrow and injustice. In these two approaches there was no contradiction and hence despite their differences they loved each other, respected each other, and worked together.

Following Gandhiji's upfront announcement that Jawaharlal Nehru would be his successor, the Hindutva brigade concluded that now they had two targets. If the truth be told, there was no pressure on Gandhiji to

---

[3]Excerpted from paper read by Prof Alok Bajpai at Pandit Nehru's fiftieth Death Centenary Conference at Jawaharlal Nehru University, May 2014, New Delhi.

declare his 'successor'. It was unwarranted, in that sense. The steps towards independence (and Partition) were far off still. The Quit India movement was launched when the Second World War was at its peak. This was not a coincidence. The Nazi forces were facing stiff resistance in Stalingrad (now Volgograd) and Russia, but overall, Hitler appeared to be conquering vast parts of Europe. There was a veritable panic and chaos, not only in Europe, but all over British colonies. Japan had captured Singapore. On 8 March 1942, Japanese forces occupied Rangoon. Japan's victories and their slogan 'Asia for Asiatics' was gaining momentum in the Indian middle classes. Germany's march in Europe and Japan's march in Asia were being celebrated by many Congressmen as well. The British wanted Indian volunteers in the army to join Britain's war effort and wanted the Congress to campaign for them. Nehru had taken a firm position that India would support the British and the Allies, but on its own terms, and that Indians would help as independent Indians. Despite the considerable popularity of Subhas Chandra Bose all over India, Nehru had stood his ground.

The Congress under Gandhiji and Nehru could not be roped in to join the British war effort. But many other political parties or organizations, from the communists to the RSS were ready to compromise with the British rulers. For communists, the Second World War had become a global people's war after the Nazi invasion of Soviet Russia. An alliance was formed between Britain, Russia and America. The RSS was not part of the Freedom Movement and had opposed the

Congress and the Gandhi-Nehru leadership. So they were closer to the British than to the independence movement.

But the war and the Japanese successes did bring the ideological and political differences into sharp focus. Michael Edwardes gives a chilling picture of the contradictions that surfaced in the Freedom Movement. He writes in his well-known political biography of Nehru, 'What was happening was almost inconceivable. The British Empire, so unyielding to Indian nationalism, was crumbling before the attacks of the Japanese. It seemed to many that Subhas Bose had been right, non-violence had only hindered the march to freedom. Yet in many ways the imminence of deliverance by the Japanese was not taken seriously. The Muslim League was more concerned with fighting Congress. The extreme communalist organization, the Hindu Mahasabha, defied the Muslims to come out and fight in the streets. As the Japanese marched on, the politicians screeched at one another. India, in Nehru's words was caught up in the "mad world of war and politics and fascism and imperialism".'[4]

The point to note is that despite Nehru's total dedication to the Mahatma and his own worldview which was against fascism and colonialism, he was not in a commanding position, even while launching the Quit India movement. He was not even convinced of the timing of it. But once the movement was launched,

[4]Michael Edwardes, *Nehru: A Political Biography*, Pelican Books, UK, 1973, p.140.

rather suddenly (though Gandhiji had been toying with such an idea for some time), it gave mixed signals to various groups within the Congress and those outside the Congress system. In that no-holds-barred situation, the movement degenerated into a sort of anarchy and violence when all the Congress leaders were arrested.

Nehru spent his longest continuous time in prison following his arrest in the 1942 Quit India movement which was started by Gandhiji almost unilaterally with a kind of desperate ultimatum of 'Do or Die'. The movement lost its momentum after a few months. Then came a long political vacuum. In this vacuum the seeds of Partition were sown. And when the leaders were released and the Second World War was over, the stage was set for the showdown—Partition and holocaust.

It was against this backdrop that the idea of killing the entire Congress leadership, particularly Gandhi (having failed twice earlier) and Nehru began to be discussed in the fanatic Hindutva groups, inspired by the RSS and HMS. But the fanatic fringe had over-estimated the differences between Gandhiji and Nehru and under-estimated the sentiment and support in favour of the party. Not only them, but even Muhammad Ali Jinnah had not understood the emotional and political depth of the Gandhi-Nehru relationship and the confidence they had in each other.

Both the Hindutva brigade and the Muslim League had convinced themselves that history was on their side. They thought they could blackmail Gandhiji and Nehru. Within the Congress there were people who were sympathetic to the Hindu idea of India. And

Jinnah had convinced a large number of his followers that Congress was essentially a Hindu party and if independence came with Gandhiji-Nehru at the helm, then the Muslims would be second-class citizens. The only option for the Muslims was to have their own country. The British were systematically encouraging the Muslim League and massaging Jinnah's large ego.

The political canvas was at once frightening and frustrating: the raging war in Europe, British economy at its lowest level of confidence, the advancing Japanese forces and vulnerable Indian borders, Subhas Chandra Bose thundering on the radio and getting a passionate response from the masses, Jinnah raising the pitch on Muslim nationalism, the Hindutva forces becoming more and more aggressive, the Congress leadership in jails and disconnected, the people of India in a political wilderness and yet still retaining their faith in the overall leadership of Gandhiji and Nehru. This was the backdrop that had begun to shape Nehru's ideas of independent India's foreign policy. His books and letters to his daughter Indira Gandhi, *Glimpses of World History* and *The Discovery of India* were reflections of his own evolving thinking about the 'Idea of India' that he envisaged. By killing Gandhiji and by plotting to kill Nehru, the Hindutva brigade was actually planning to kill that glorious, global and grand vision of India. People had begun to see their dreams and hopes in Nehru.

Nehru's communication with the masses was direct. There was no TV and even the penetration of radio was limited. The only medium was the press and its reach was primarily around the cities. Even telephones were very few and only the rich or privileged had them. Mobile phones, the Internet and the whole gigantic network of social media was not even a distant technological dream. And yet, Pandit Nehru's image, personality and charm were palpably felt all over the country—from remote villages in Karnataka to the valley of Kashmir.

The new class, or rather new caste, currently called 'NRI' was yet to emerge. Going abroad (mainly to England in those days) was a matter of great prestige and luck. The elite in India had all their icons or reference points in the UK—be they cricketers or writers. America had yet to enter middle-class consciousness. Nehru did not have to go for any gimmicks or image-building exercises to be in the hearts of the people. Neither a broom nor Madison Square Garden were required for a carefully crafted photo-op.

Nehru would be at ease with scientists, English and Hindi writers and poets, intellectuals and statesmen, and equally at home with tribals and farmers or factory workers. There was no higher middle class which could flaunt its unearned wealth. There were a few traditionally rich families and a small layer of aristocracy. The term middle class was essentially used to describe white collar employees, teachers and the upper caste layer. All people, irrespective of class, caste, region or religion were enamoured of Panditji.

There were critics of Nehru, of course, from pro-capitalist lawyer, activist and politician C. Rajagopalachari (later the last Governor-General of India), to hard-core socialist Ram Manohar Lohia. But even the critics and detractors used to be overwhelmed by Nehru's speeches and his towering presence. Lakhs of people thronged just to see and hear him talk about the threats of communalism, of superstitious ideas, of sectarian and divisive forces in society.

What was the secret of Jawaharlal Nehru's charisma? How could he attract and influence the poor peasants in Uttar Pradesh and Bihar and also the newly educated middle class? How could he dazzle young scientists and technocrats by his reason and vision? How could he influence global leaders? He argued passionately for the human rights of people oppressed by colonialism and imperialism. He talked of the eradication of global poverty and backwardness. He stood by Arab nationalism and Palestine's freedom. The whole emerging political leadership of the Third World as well as Europe was in thrall of Pandit Nehru. His idealism, dedication to the cause of freedom, his courageous confrontation of decadent and obscurantist ideas, his faith in science and his faith in the basic goodness and virtue of people, his pacifist philosophy and commitment to social justice, his love for nature, his zest for mountaineering and trekking, his love for poetry and philosophy were so transparent that he never had to make them into cheap exercises in event management.

Nehru's visits to Sri Aurobindo's ashram in Pondicherry and Rabindranath Tagore's university in Shantiniketan, the Theosophical Society's headquarters in Adyar and Bharatpur's forests used to become events simply because he went there. He was totally involved with Indian and Western philosophy as well as Buddhist texts and Islamic civilization. That was his secularism. It was respect for human civilizations, which included religion and science.

After Independence, Nehru further expanded his huge network, as it were. His discussions with artists and his visits to art galleries, his attendance at avant garde theatre, would be the talk of the town, whether the town was London, or his alma mater Cambridge, or Delhi or Bangalore. His dialogue with legendary filmmakers like Satyajit Ray and Bimal Roy, with K.A. Abbas and V. Shantaram, his appreciation of Dilip Kumar and Raj Kapoor inspired the whole film industry. He did not have to 'invite' the film artistes to join his campaign and enlarge his ego. It was at his initiative that the Film Institute of Pune, the Sahitya Akademi and National School of Drama were created, and later flourished under the personal attention of Indira Gandhi. Nehru became a legend in his own lifetime.

His detractors tried to belittle him by comparing him with Vallabhbhai Patel or Subhas Chandra Bose. For Nehru, they were comrades-in-arms. In spite of the political and ideological differences, he had immense respect and affection for all those who were tirelessly working towards the cause of freedom and building a modern India. It is sad indeed to see him compared and run down vis-à-vis his fellow satyagrahis and followers of Mahatma Gandhi. No matter how tall the statues built for other great leaders may be, Pandit Jawaharlal Nehru will remain much taller than them. He was not just the first prime minister. He was a world leader and a *deep-stambha* for human civilization.

On a visit to Pakistan for a conference, I struck up a conversation with the driver who had come to escort me to the airport. Pakistan was then under the military rule of General Pervez Musharraf. I asked my escort how it felt to be under military dictatorship. He replied that he truly envied India. 'If Pakistan had Nehru or somebody like him to lead, we would not be so miserable.' He added that Pakistan lost the script within a decade of Partition, when 'you had a great liberal democrat to lead you and we were cursed to have a military dictatorship'.

But unfortunately, India seems to have lost the script now. The liberal Indian is becoming an intolerant Indian. Instead of being proud of secular internationalism, many in the intelligentsia have begun to shout '*garv se kaho hum Hindu hain*' (say with pride that we are Hindus). Now, even in Parliament, one hears speeches glorifying medieval India's decadent values. Indeed, the term 'secular' is either ridiculed or even used as a term of abuse. Instead of a scientific temper, it is now fashionable to glorify absurd and superstitious customs, in the name of 'tradition'. Identitarian politics has replaced ideological discourse. Idealism is passé now and cynicism is in vogue. The media often behaves like a monster. History is being rewritten to suit the prejudices and whims of the new rulers. But they are not just prejudices and whims—there is a method in the emerging madness. It is not just the Planning Commission that was demolished. They want to erase the grand Discovery of India and her Tryst with Destiny and replace it with the Rediscovery of Medieval India and her Tryst with Despondency!

The Many Faces of Jawaharlal

Aakar Patel

Leaders of politics tend to come to us in one or two dimensions. One reason is that they have spent many decades of their lives doing the same thing, and politics on the subcontinent is not a part-time profession. Indeed, successful politicians who come up from the local level all need to set aside their personal lives to attend to the everyday problems of their constituents—from school admissions and electricity bills to police cases—in an astonishingly busy schedule that never really relents. As the leader rises up the ranks this petitioning from the local resident with his local problems ends. But he is replaced now by members of the party, by businessmen, by bureaucrats and so on, all of whom are also there for the personal intervention of the leader.

Given all of this, and this format of politics is no different anywhere in the country, there is no real space for a personal life and no time for hobbies or for reading. This produces the one-dimensional leader, no matter how talented or promising in other respects. A second reason, and this is likely more applicable to our politicians and therefore a more cruel observation, is that politics tends to repel certain sorts of people because of its rough-and-tumble aspects. It is the rare and unusual man or woman who is truly enlightened that ventures into this field. It is just too raw and demanding in its practice for someone accustomed to domains that are more civilized than the party office. There are some exceptions to this rule and usually they tend to come from certain backgrounds.

Leaders who are parachuted into high-level politics because of their family power, for instance Rajiv Gandhi and his son Rahul and wife Sonia, or because of their qualities, such as economist Manmohan Singh, have more opportunity to be different. They have had the space before their life in politics to develop another side that might add to their functions as a leader. But if we scan the horizon for leaders with additional and unusual qualities we usually look in vain. The one man who stands out, who is so different from the others so as to be in a category by himself, is Jawaharlal Nehru.

As a leader he was cast in the mould, if it be a mould, of Thomas Jefferson. America's third president was a man with deep interest in many things. His day began with a recording of the atmospheric pressure and the temperature at his residence, Monticello (designed by Jefferson himself, under the influence of the work of the neo-classical architect Palladio, in Charlottesville in the Piedmont region of the state of Virginia). His library had over 5,000 volumes and his range of interests was magnificent.

In 1962, when he threw a party for forty-nine Nobel Laureates, President John F. Kennedy said: 'I think this is the most extraordinary collection of talent, of human knowledge…ever gathered at the White House, with the possible exception of when Thomas Jefferson dined alone.' Something similar may be said about Nehru.

He was the sort of man whom Socrates would have appreciated as the ideal Platonic philosopher-king, though, and this is an important qualification, Nehru detested autocracies. His views on this, and his writing pseudonymous letters condemning himself, are well known and need not detain us here. What is important is that he was possessed of these ideals without deliberate effort and without wanting to be either philosopher or king.

Some of Nehru's letters from jail to his daughter Indira Gandhi have been compiled as the work *Glimpses of World History*. It carries the modest subtitle 'Being further letters to his daughter written in prison and containing a rambling account of history for young people'. It is in fact a book that should be required reading in all of our schools at the primary level for what history is and how it is to be written. He wrote the book in bits, and this results in an advantage because it shows his astonishing range, even if he himself dismisses it as 'rambling'. Nehru was relying on his memory and some of his fellow inmates for dates. I think it was Abul Kalam Azad, a man of formidable retention, who supplied much of the chronological sequencing.[1]

How many world leaders can write fluently and without resource about medieval India, the qualities of Akbar, French dominance over Europe, Ataturk's Turkey and the reasons for Mongol success? I cannot think of many from India other than B.R. Ambedkar, and, sadly, I cannot name any of our prime ministers as being capable of doing what Nehru did. He engaged with and understood the world in a way that most people even in his family did not. It is difficult to align the frankly primitive way in which Rajiv Gandhi, Indira Gandhi and Sonia Gandhi think and behave with the giant who was their forebear.

Nehru's brilliance and width did not come from academic excellence alone, and here he is different from two leaders who are former academics and similar in their styles, Barack Obama and Manmohan Singh. Nehru is not like them, and indeed, he did not do particularly well at Cambridge.

It was his interests outside of what he was occupied with that make him such an interesting man. One of his biographers, the Australian Walter Crocker, tells us that: 'There were two men in Dr Jekyll and Mr Hyde; there were more like twenty in Nehru.'

Where can we begin to look at his many sides? Let us begin with what he has left behind on the educational side. Without Nehru we would not have the Indian Institutes of Technology (IITs) and the Indian Institutes

---

[1]Abul Kalam Azad (1888-1958) was a scholar and political leader in the forefront of the independence movement. He was India's first minister of education after Independence.

of Management (IIMs) in the way that they have come down to us. We would not have, in all probability, such places as the National Institute of Design (NID) either and it is remarkable that these retain their dominance in their respective fields so many decades after Nehru has gone.

Why is this so? Even a leader as talented as Manmohan Singh could only add to the IITs and IIMs in his time as prime minister. We have not had someone come up with the idea of, say, a network of institutions that train Indians in first-rate blue collar work. We have crude attempts to do this but nothing that is of the quality of the IITs and the reason is that after Nehru we can duplicate his ideas and implement his vision but not come up with original things of our own.

Or look at culture. Nehru was president of the Sahitya Akademi, the National Academy of Letters devoted to the promotion of literature in all Indian languages, and took deep interest in its work and even in its awardees, whose work presumably he would have been familiar with. It is not easy to think of any leader after him and particularly our last prime minister, Singh, and the current one, Narendra Modi, as being interested enough in such things so as to be head of the Akademi. Modi's interests in culture end with cricket and he was while chief minister of Gujarat also the head of the state's cricket board, giving him a say in the Board of Control for Cricket in India (BCCI). For a leader who enthusiastically wants to engage with the writing and art of others we must look to Nehru.

Going through his selected works one afternoon

(an exercise that is inevitably rewarding and one that I recommend strongly to readers), I came across this note that Nehru wrote to the then Union Minister for Information and Broadcasting, B.V. Keskar, along with an enclosed letter: 'I have been rather worried at the progressive disappearance of Western music from India. Bombay is practically the only centre left, where this is encouraged. I think Indian music will profit by contacts with Western music. I know nothing about the person who has written this letter. But, as there appear to be few Indians who have studied Western music, I feel a little interested in him.'

The content of that letter is unknown, but its writer was Adi J. Desai, a Parsi. Nehru's worry was justified, though he was optimistic in assuming that Western classical music would survive the exit of the British. Fifty years later, it is dead everywhere in India except South Bombay. And here it is dying as one community depopulates. But the interesting thing is the level at which Nehru engages with the subject. It is obvious that he hasn't merely 'forwarded' it to 'the concerned person' as happens in our time, but actually thought about it.

The other interesting thing is that the letter is from May 1957, a decade after Nehru had been leading India and at a time when a lot must have been occupying both his mind and his schedule. But to him this was important.

Unlike most urban Indians, Nehru was a naturalist. He took great joy in putting together a garden in his official residence. He could identify trees and flowers, according to those who knew him, and he kept a whole zoo of animals inside the house including pandas. It is these various interests of his that produced the man who could gift us institutions whose quality required more than just funding. They required real vision and Nehru, more than any other leader we have had, possessed this in abundance.

This came to him not through his academic studies, as I have already referred to earlier. Crocker says he was instinctively brilliant. He once took a biologist, who had won the Nobel Prize, to Nehru. At their meeting, Crocker says, the scientist 'made a careless remark about some work. Nehru pounced on it, politely, and demolished it. This was typical. Few errors in reasoning escaped him'.

Being a man of such intelligence and sensitivity, Nehru did not necessarily love the behaviour of the Indians whom he met. Where he could not influence or change such behaviour he would shame people into following him. For instance, once at a parade in Delhi, some Congressmen were objecting loudly to being seated on the grass instead of on chairs. Nehru did not respond to them but got off his chair and himself sat on the grass, silencing them all immediately. Similarly, at a reception where MPs began littering the ground with banana peels and wrappers, Nehru himself began cleaning the ground, getting them to behave likewise.

One of the most revealing paragraphs about Nehru is this one which opens Crocker's book: 'I first saw Nehru in 1945. At the time I was serving in the British army, and the end of the war happened to find me in

India for a while before demobilization. Nehru had not been long out of prison and was making a triumphal tour in Bengal. Crowds gathered to see him at the railway station in my area; huge and enthusiastic crowds. I noticed at the station where I was waiting for him that his evident satisfaction at the crowd's welcome did not prevent him from impatiently pushing—some of my brother officers said slapping—people who got too near him.'

It is perfectly true that Nehru was irritable, but he was also bombastic and verbose, making too many speeches (often three a day) and spending too much time lecturing the West. He was careless with his time, once giving three hours to a high school delegation from Australia, while his ministers waited outside.

These were of course teenagers but it would surprise many people that the Chacha Nehru who loved little children was apparently a myth and Nehru did not really have time for or enjoy the company of children. To quote Crocker, 'Nehru certainly did some acting on public occasions and before TV cameras...The acting was never worse than the pose of Chacha Nehru with the children. This was at its worst on his birthday for a few years when sycophants organized groups of children, with flowers and copious photographing, to parade with him. It was out of character; his interest in children was slender.' In my opinion this clichéd typecasting of him has taken away from many people real knowledge of his angularities and interesting facets.

Crocker thought Nehru 'had no sympathy for Gandhi's religion, or for religiousness at all'. But there is a photograph in Mushirul Hasan's *The Nehrus* that shows Jawaharlal entering the Ganga wearing a janoi, the Brahmin's sacred thread. The thread looks new, however, and it's not visible in two other photographs of him bare-chested, one in swimming trunks and the other doing shirshasan, the headstand practised by followers of yoga.

I think Nehru engaged with the culture but did not succumb to it. He was an Indian and proud of being one, as his magnificent work *The Discovery of India* (another text that is not but should be made compulsory reading in our schools) shows. But he did not feel the need, as do many leaders including our current one, to find security in the symbolism (tikas, turbans and so on) of religion.

Some other aspects of Nehru are revealed through anecdotes. He did not dismiss those who came to him with petitions and while they waited for their turn to meet him they were not chased away. He had great tolerance and patience for the poor and he allowed a slum to slowly come up right in front of the prime minister's house, sympathizing with its occupants rather than turning the police on them. Such things reveal the man, and we can safely rule out any of our leaders doing this. The sanitized localities they live in and sanitized corridors they travel in are far removed from Nehru's acceptance of the facts and his decision not to turn his eye away from the reality of India.

Nehru had great physical courage. We know this from the famous story of an incident during the riots of Partition in Delhi. Nehru was already prime minister when he was passing by a mob that was attacking a Muslim tailor at Chandni Chowk. He ordered the car to stop and jumped in to save the man, swinging a lathi that he took from the police. He had no care for his personal safety and of course this was in the time when prime ministers did not have the sort of security that they do today. But he thought of nothing other than the victim and the mob, terrified at the enraged leader in their midst, fled.

Nehru was dyed secular through and through. It was not something that he put on. It is said that he rejected advice to remove the Muslim cooks in his kitchen because he refused to see all individuals through the lens of their faith. Every generation is fortunate to have such a man leading them and Gandhi knew what he was doing when he trained and gifted Nehru to us.

It is always breathtaking to assess Nehru and look at the scale of his ambition. One of his biographers, the Congressman Shashi Tharoor, has written that while he was going through the drudgery of daily work (a prime minister also never really escapes that political life described in the opening lines of this essay), Nehru also always had an eye on the horizon, at the future and what was possible. This optimism of his has produced for us in middle-class India today, with all of our opportunities, about as much as an individual could have left as an inheritance while leading a country with almost no resources.

Another of Nehru's biographers, the Bharatiya Janata Party's spokesman M.J. Akbar, says that Nehru's 'most important contribution in a life full of contributions was a clear establishment of a vision in which to lift India from the eighteenth century towards the twenty-first. One of the things that we underestimate in governance or public life is the commitment to the future. Governance very often becomes a matter of tackling day-to-day management, particularly in a complex country like ours.'

Whereas Nehru saw it also as addressing the future. It is these aspects, these facets that inform Nehru the leader and statesmen.

It is almost fashionable to see Nehru as a clueless old fogey who sentimentally preferred 'Nehruvian socialism' to a fabulous capitalism that could have brought India out of poverty. Whether this is true and whether the alternative will succeed as many think it will, remains to be seen.

But the reduction of Nehru as if he were innocently idealistic about socialism or ignorant of the capacity and the ability of the state is wrong. We have to consider why he was so brutally realistic about Kashmir, and why against his democratic instinct, he declined to let Kashmiris have their plebiscite. Nehru's annexation of Goa was illegal, though only C. Rajagopalachari and Jayaprakash Narayan opposed it. Crocker writes what many of us will not believe: If Portugal had insisted on a plebiscite, Goans would have preferred Portuguese rule to Indian. Nehru was clear-minded enough to be able to see this and we should not buy the allegation that he was muddle-headed about much larger things such as the economy.

Perhaps it is for this reason that Nehru is seen with warmth despite his many failures. He was a good man, who meant well and meant to do well, and he did.

The Truth-teller

Hartosh Bal

As a child of the 1960s, I belong to the first generation that did not see any of the leaders of the independence movement up close. Growing up, we only inherited the sense of awe that still lingered around their names. The cynicism with which we can today talk of Mahatma Gandhi and Jawaharlal Nehru was a product of later times, perhaps triggered off by the excesses of the Emergency.

Much of what was passed on to us through textbooks and on occasions such as Gandhi Jayanti and Children's Day verged on the hagiographic. It was difficult to take this seriously, so my first sense of Nehru came from my father, in particular, and my uncle, both IPS (Indian Police Service) officers. My father was no theoretician of secularism, he was a hard-nosed cop in Madhya Pradesh at a time when policing was about getting things done on the ground, whether it involved tackling dacoity in the Chambal or student unrest in Jabalpur.

This was a time of minimum connectivity, road or phone, between the outlying areas and the district headquarters, and sometimes between the district headquarters and the state capital. It ensured considerable autonomy, and a wealth of anecdotage and experience that bureaucrats today seem to lack. I delayed my desire to record these stories once too often, so today I am left with impressions rather than anecdotage. Among the impressions I gathered from my father, one that has stayed with me is that with the passing of Nehru something vital was lost to the country.

Perhaps, all my subsequent reading of Nehru has been coloured by this fact. Over the years I have read much that has been written about Nehru by biographers such as Sarvepalli Gopal, chroniclers such as M.J. Akbar, elucidators of his contribution to the making of modern India such as Sunil Khilnani and Ramachandra Guha. But it is my reading of Nehru's own writings that has left the deepest impression.

This is not the case with, for example, Gandhi. For all the adulation the country has bestowed on Gandhi, I find him a difficult figure to warm up to. Recent attempts to portray him as a New Age saint do nothing to change this. My feeling is that the magic of Gandhi lay in the man, and it is difficult for those who never had any personal contact with him to comprehend what he represented. On the strength of his writings, he comes across as an obdurate and self-centred man given to ideas of diet and sex that seemed to be born out of his belief that the body of the nation was reflected in his body, and if he could only control and coerce his body to his will, the nation would follow suit.

The difference between the two today is that, unlike

Gandhi, Nehru continues to be easily accessible. If Gandhi comes across as a cantankerous sage, Nehru is clearly a child of modernity, a fact readily apparent in what I believe is a significant and underrated book—*The Discovery of India*.

Perhaps, it is best to begin a defence of this book, and hence of Nehru with an old Indian tradition, of presenting the *pratipaksh*, the strongest argument against the claim. In his recent essays, 'Why Partition?' and 'After Nehru', in the *London Review of Books*, the Marxist historian Perry Anderson writes, 'His most ambitious work, *The Discovery of India*, which appeared in 1946, is a steam bath of *Schwärmerei*. *The Discovery of India*… illustrates not just Nehru's lack of formal scholarship and addiction to romantic myth, but something deeper, not so much an intellectual as a psychological limitation: a capacity for self-deception with far-reaching political consequences.'

Let us leave aside the larger irony of a Marxist, with a belief in the objective and material conditions, making so much of an individual's influence, and consider the charge. *Schwärmerei*, meaning excessive sentiment or enthusiasm, is one of those words foreign to English which have no essential need to be used in a text except to signal an author's erudition. The accusation is that sentimentality and flights of fancy envelop the book to the point that its contents are self-deceptive.

Nehru's prose is indeed overwrought and this sometimes takes away from the arguments being made. But even so, for me the *Discovery* provides the most compelling take on the history of India that I have encountered, marred by none of the nationalistic sensibilities that contort histories written after Partition, whether communal or secular.

Anderson notes the date of the book's publication, 1946, but does not bother to observe its significance. India is on the verge of independence, and the man who is all but certain to be prime minister has published a book which shows a complete awareness of the deprivation that colonialism has inflicted on us. Yet, it is not an angry or a denunciatory book, and it betrays no hatred of the people who will soon walk away from the subcontinent.

Somewhere towards the middle of this vast sweep of history Nehru meditates on the establishment of the British Empire: 'Looking back over this period, it almost seems that the British succeeded in dominating India by a succession of fortuitous circumstances and lucky flukes…And yet a closer scrutiny reveals, in the circumstances, then existing, a certain inevitability in what happened.'

Nehru titled this section, 'The Backwardness of the Indian and Superiority of the English in Organization and Technique'. This, perhaps, is all that needs to be said. The inevitability of what transpired lay in this superiority of technique, which was not restricted to the military but extended to all spheres of government—administrative and economic.

Interestingly, the superiority of technique was itself the product of fortuitous circumstances and lucky flukes in Europe but the British internalized it. For them, this superiority was a corollary of their being a superior race.

It was an attitude that was in some measure common to all European colonial powers, and eventually this categorization of an entire people as superior or inferior returned to haunt Europe under the guise of the Nazis.

In the centuries that this attitude lasted, and its vestiges have still not disappeared, those who were at the receiving end reacted in various fashion to this imposed humiliation. Among them it created intellectual distortions, a defensiveness about their past, about their very selves. We are still living with the results. The RSS (Rashtriya Swayamsevak Sangh) is the result of just such a distortion. The desire to invoke a glorious past, to lay claim to all knowledge, in particular the scientific knowledge that seemed to lie behind the success of the colonizers, was a consequence of this feeling of being victimized.

The term *Ressentiment* (a foreign word that is not easily replaced, unlike *Schwärmerei*, but loosely translated as a sense of hostility towards the perceived cause of one's frustration), central to Nietzsche's writings, denotes the nature of this phenomenon. The RSS's worldview has internalized the idea of defeat by colonial powers, and now seeks refuge in hostility at everything suggestive of that defeat. The RSS's hatred of Christianity and Islam is only a manifestation of a much larger malaise.

Ironically, if the RSS had truly looked at their own heritage they may have escaped the trap they find themselves in. For Nietzsche, the Buddha's great strength lay in his victory over *Ressentiment*, 'Not by enmity is enmity ended.' It is a belief that underlay Gandhi's approach to the independence movement, which was never directed against the individuals in India who represented the Raj but the institutions and laws that made colonial rule possible.

Nehru had little patience with Gandhi's fads, or his romanticization of village life but he admired the ethical core at the heart of Gandhi's actions. And I do think, with the distance my generation has been granted from these events, that the lack of *Ressentiment* that Gandhi shared with Nehru was by far the more important consideration in his choosing Nehru over any other possible successor. In turn Nehru brought this same lack of *Ressentiment* to how he conducted the politics of independent India. The decision to join the Commonwealth is just one such example.

In the *Discovery* Nehru seems to suggest a far more reasonable approach to Gandhi's belief that the search for the nation's failings may lie in his body. He searches instead for answers to our current failings in the changing body-politic of the subcontinent, 'What is my inheritance? To what am I an heir? To all that humanity has achieved during tens of thousands of years...But there is a special heritage for those of us in India...one more especially applicable to us, something that is in our flesh and blood and bones, that has gone to make us what we are and what we are likely to be.'

This is the thread that holds together the book, which early on carries a caution about an uncritical look at our past: 'A country under foreign domination seeks escape from the present in dreams of a vanished age, and finds consolation in visions of past greatness. This is a foolish and dangerous pastime in which many of us indulge. An equally questionable practice for us in India is to imagine that we are still spiritually great though we have come down in the world in other respects. Spiritual or any other greatness cannot be founded on lack of freedom and opportunity, or on starvation and misery.'

His diagnosis of the Indian condition follows soon after the caution, and it takes the form of a quote from Aurobindo, 'If an ancient Indian of the time of the Upanishad, of the Buddha, or the later classical age were to be set down in modern India…he would see his race clinging to forms and shells and rags of the past and missing nine-tenths of its nobler meaning…he would be amazed by the extent of the mental poverty, the immobility, the static repetition, the cessation of science, the long sterility of art, the comparative feebleness of the creative intuition.'

Nehru locates the beginning of this decay to the end of the classical era, 'During the first thousand years of the Christian era, there are many ups and downs in India, many conflicts with invading elements and internal troubles. Yet, it is a period of vigorous national life, bubbling over with energy and spreading out in all directions. Culture develops into a rich civilization flowering out in philosophy, literature, drama, art, science and mathematics.'

Yet this flowering enters a period of slow decline, 'There is no great figure in philosophy after Shankara in the eighth century…In literature, Bhavabuti (eighth century) is the last great figure…In mathematics, Bhaskara II (twelfth century) is the last great name…'

From these observations, he reaches a conclusion which is remarkable in overturning one of the key misconceptions about our past, 'Radhakrishnan says that Indian philosophy lost its vigour with the loss of political freedom...But why should political freedom be lost unless some kind of decay has preceded it? A small country might easily be overwhelmed by superior power, but a huge well-developed and highly civilized country cannot succumb to external attack unless there is internal decay, or the invader possesses a higher technique of warfare. That internal decay is clearly evident in India at the close of these thousand years.'

The fault is not in external events, but in us. And what is the nature of this fault? Nehru answers, 'The Indian social structure...had given amazing stability to Indian civilization...So long as the structure afforded avenues for growth and expansion, it was progressive; when it reached the limits of expansion open to it, it became stationary, unprogressive, and later, inevitably regressive. Because of this there was decline along the line—intellectual, philosophical, political, in technique and methods of warfare, in knowledge and contacts with the outside world...'

This internal decay is, in Nehru's view, key to the decline that leads to colonialism, and the often decried advent of Islam does not contribute to the decay but rather shores up a tottering civilization for a few extra centuries: '...in north India cultural decay was very evident. Fixed beliefs and a rigid social structure prevented social effort and advance. The coming of Islam and of a considerable number of people from outside, with different ways of living and thought, affected existing beliefs and structure. A foreign conquest, with all its evils, has one advantage: it widens the mental horizon of the people and compels them to look out of their shells…There were many changes in India and new impulses brought freshness and life to art and architecture and other cultural patterns.'

Again Nehru's clear-headedness is remarkable. The medieval synthesis that we tend to exalt could not completely reverse the decay that had set in, 'And yet all this was the result of two old-world patterns coming into contact, both of which had lost their initial vitality and creative vigour and were set in rigid frames. Indian culture was very old and tired, the Arab-Persian culture had long passed its zenith and the old curiosity and sense of mental adventure which distinguished the Arabs was no more in evidence.'

Even Akbar, the emperor we have come to see as some sort of symbol of medieval greatness, was blind to the advances that were underway in Europe at the same time. 'Akbar was full of curiosity, ever seeking to find out about things, both spiritual and temporal. He was interested in mechanical contrivances and in the science of war…And yet it is very odd how his curiosity stopped at a point and did not lead him to explore certain obvious avenues which lay open before him. With all his prestige as the Great Mughal and the strength of his empire as a land power, he was powerless at sea…He did think of building ships once, but this was looked upon more as a pastime than a serious naval development…in matters of artillery the Mughal armies, as well as those of other states in India at the time chiefly relied on foreign experts...but why didn't Akbar or anyone else send his own men abroad for training or interest himself in improvement by encouraging research work?...The Jesuits presented Akbar with a printed Bible and perhaps one or two other printed books. Why did he not get curious about printing...?'

Few essential details escape Nehru. He goes on to write about the Sikh emperor Ranjit Singh, and his curiosity, a term that takes on remarkable importance in Nehru's view of history. Ranjit Singh's curiosity does indeed take him where Akbar did not go, the training of his troops on a European model and the development of his own artillery on a scale superior to that of the British, but even he did not imbibe an essential lesson. European technique was not meant to be implemented piecemeal; it had to extend from the army to the civil administration. The feudal modes of inheritance of the kingdom after Ranjit Singh's death led to the collapse of the short-lived Sikh empire.

This feudal element continued to reside in the native states the British had carved out of India. Nehru's language may be given to romanticism but his view of Indian history was not, he would have little time for the mythology many modern Indian historians have built around the 1857 Mutiny in the years since Independence. Nehru notes, 'The revolt of 1857-58 was essentially a feudal uprising, though there were some nationalistic elements in it.'

Instead Nehru sees the Mutiny as a point of departure which contains the seeds of much that followed later.

The preponderance of Muslims among the feudal class was the product of the Mughal domination of India, and what was once a source of power and privilege became a handicap in the aftermath of the Mutiny: 'Of necessity, British rule had to be accepted, but the break with the past had brought something more than a new government; it had brought doubt and confusion and a loss of faith in themselves. That break indeed had come long before the Mutiny, and had led to the many movements of thought in Bengal and elsewhere...But the Muslims generally had retired into their shell far more than the Hindus, avoided Western education, and lived in day-dreams of a restoration of the old order.'

The consequence of such an attitude was, Nehru writes, that '[t]here has been a difference of a generation or more in the development of the Hindu and Muslim middle classes, and the difference continues to show itself in many directions, political, economic, and other. It is this lag that produces a psychology of fear among the Muslims.'

It is interesting to note that the language in its attribution of cause and effect is old-fashioned but that does not change the fact that these observations can be recast and backed with enough evidence to meet the standards of rigour that would satisfy the Marxist historian in Anderson.

Having made this observation, Nehru concludes, almost prophetically, 'Pakistan, the proposal to divide India, however much it may appeal emotionally to some, is of course no solution for this backwardness, and it is much more likely to strengthen the hold of feudal elements for some time longer and delay the economic progress of the Muslims.'

He goes on to describe an encounter which I believe has been quoted far less than it deserves, 'Iqbal was one of the early advocates of Pakistan and yet he appears to have realized its inherent danger and absurdity...A few months before his death, as he lay on his sick bed, he sent for me and I gladly obeyed the summons. As I talked to him about many things I felt that how much we had in common, in spite of differences, and how easy it was to get on with him. He was in a reminiscent mood, and wandered from one subject to another, and I listened to him, talking little myself. I admired him and his poetry, and it pleased me greatly to feel that he liked me and had a good opinion of me: "What is there in common between Jinnah and you? He is a politician and you are a patriot."'

In our times we place little value on a patriot willing to speak the truth to us. The history of India by Nehru is not a history of rancour or impotence, as the RSS would have it, nor is it a history of syncretism that was marred only by the arrival of the British, as many nationalist historians would have it. It is not history that lionizes either Rana Pratap or Akbar, the failings of both were apparent to him. Well before the medieval period, Nehru felt, classical India had become ossified, damned by the very social structure that gave it stability.

This understanding of the past came with a clear realization that it did not hold answers to what lay ahead for the sub-continent: 'Some Hindus talk of going back to the Vedas; some Muslims dream of an

Islamic theocracy. Idle fancies, for there is no going back to the past...'

The directions that Nehru chose for this country after Independence make sense only in light of his view of our history. One of them impelled him to do away with the ossified social structure that still shackled the country. Another to ensure we mastered the techniques that won the subcontinent for the British in the first place.

The stress on technique explains the thrust on the IITs (Indian Institutes of Technology) and the IIMs (Indian Institutes of Management) in the early years of Independence. Its results are evident today. India has the finest pool of technical and managerial manpower outside the Western world. The question of what use this manpower is put to now cannot be laid at Nehru's door. Technique does not come with an intrinsic set of values; it serves colonialism as easily as it serves a liberal state. In our case the values technique should subscribe to, even if we overlook this fact, are part of the Constitution, which is as much Nehru's work as it is of B.R. Ambedkar.

These two also came together to redress the question of our ossified social structure. The passage of the Hindu code bills in the 1950s remains one of the major achievements of our democracy. Ambedkar quit the Cabinet well before they were passed, upset with Nehru's push to the reforms in their entirety. But without Nehru none of these reforms would have ever become reality. Ambedkar on his own could not have taken on the Hindu Right. In fact, without

Nehru the Hindu Right would have been the dominant influence in India right from the country's inception. Given this, it is ironical that today there are enough to speak for Ambedkar or for the Hindu Right, and very few for Nehru. The Congress doesn't really count, his descendants who shaped India after him may be his genetic kin but they shared no kinship of the mind.

It is a fate he seemed to have anticipated. Writing about Gandhi, he had quoted from Liddell Hart, 'History bears witness to a vital part that the "prophets" have played in human progress—which is evidence of the ultimate practical value of expressing unreservedly the truth as one sees it. Yet it has also become clear that acceptance and spreading of that vision has always depended on another class of men—"leaders" who had to be philosophical strategists, striking a compromise between truth and men's receptivity to it. Their effect has often depended on their own limitations in perceiving the truth as on their practical wisdom in proclaiming it.

'The prophets must be stoned; that is their lot, and the test of their self-fulfilment. But a leader who is stoned may merely prove that he has failed in his function through a deficiency of wisdom, or through confusing his function with that of a prophet. Time alone can tell whether the effect of such a sacrifice redeems the apparent failure as a leader that does honour to him as a man. At least he avoids the more common fault of leaders—that of sacrificing the truth to expediency without ultimate advantage to the cause. For whoever habitually suppresses the truth in the interests of tact will produce a deformity from the womb of his thought.'

A Tryst with Nehru

Shiv Visvanathan

This is a story of the Nehru era, written partly through memories of childhood. India became free in 1947 and I arrived soon after the Republic. Mahatma Gandhi and Jawaharlal Nehru made India free and, as my father told me, Gandhi and Nehru made my childhood freer. The nation and I were left to dream together. The Nehruvian era granted me that innocence as one encountered life, history, science, the world, all with a sense of enchantment.

For me, childhood is incomplete without fairytale and myth. I always felt one needed a sense of romanticism. Romanticism without secularism would have been sentimental but secularism without romanticism would have been empty. Nehru was the best combination of two concepts, not as 'isms', or ideologies but as a lived aesthetics. My father explained it beautifully. We were talking of why Gandhi picked Nehru as successor. For Appa, the choice was inevitable. Gandhi to him was the ultimate ethical man, a man who transformed ethics into politics. But Nehru was an aesthete and modernity was only sufferable as aesthetics. Modernity gave you that style, that gloss that India needed in the post-colonial era. It was a contract, a promise between the beautiful and the good to sustain the truth about India. My father added that Jayaprakash Narayan, the economist and pioneer of rural economic development theories, J.C. Kumarappa, B.R. Ambedkar, Sardar Patel were wonderful hyphens to Gandhi but Gandhi and Nehru were subject and predicate of a sentence called the nation. Only Nehru, he felt, could complete the Gandhian argument. Their differences made the complementarity complete.

India was free, Third World, non-aligned, democratic and we consumed these words like fairytales. Textbooks and adults destroy these words. One has to savour and see them through the eyes of a child. Childhood creates a hummock out of the nation. It is as if Hans Andersen rewrote Mazzini.[1] Our Constitution was like a Panchatantra tale. I saw Nehru like a Tenali Raman. These key words of politics created a sensorium, gave me a sense of good and evil. Partition jarred India. My father was born in Lahore and my parents were in Calcutta during the 1947 riots. Yet they felt freedom was a moment of healing. I contributed my happy bit by composing a joint Indo-Pakistan cricket team. Magnanimously, I let Fazal Mahmood be captain. Lala Amarnath, for all his genius, did not quite seem like leadership material and I reluctantly conceded

[1]Giuseppe Mazzini was an Italian politician, journalist and activist for the unification of Italy in the nineteenth century.

that Hanif Mohammad was the Sunil Gavaskar of the earlier era.

I was proud to be an Indian. It was like being part of the school A team which I never qualified for. For me, citizenship of a nation was easier than qualifying for a sports team. Nationalism was a bit of a boy scout movement. You took the right oaths, looked solemn in the right rituals. It felt official, like a parent-teachers meeting. In fact, Nehru was not quite official. He was Chachaji; his birthday, 14 November, was celebrated as Children's Day and was a sacrament of sweets. Nehru was part of my childhood in strange and memorable ways. I remember he had a cameo appearance in Raj Kapoor's hit movie *Ab Dilli Dur Nahin*. Doordarshan was less insufferable because of his presence. He and the philosopher Dr Sarvepalli Radhakrishnan, who was India's first vice-president and later president, added an elegance to the boring bureaucratic scripts. I remember Radhakrishnan sonorously reciting 'the role of education is to educate, to entertain and elevate the spirit of man'. I used the sentence often without quotes in my school essays. It was like living inside a fairytale without a wicked witch or demon.

I walked around as if India had invented non-alignment and I loved to watch non-alignment meets. The Panchsheel and the Bandung agreements,[2] moth-eaten today, were

[2]See p.47, footnote 19 for explanation of Panchsheel. The first large-scale Asian-African or Afro-Asian Conference—also known as the Bandung Conference—was a meeting of Asian and African states, most

music to my ears. In fact, I thought the United Nations was invented so Indian statesmen could enact their cameo roles. I waited every day to read *The Hindu*, a genuinely Nehruvian newspaper where journalists like K.S. Shelvankar, Shiva Rao, Batuk Gathani and S.K. Gurunathan captured the Nehruvian order. To me, Egyptian president Abdel Nasser, Cuban leader Fidel Castro, China's Chou en-Lai and Sukarno of Indonesia were supporting actors to the Nehruvian drama. Non-alignment was a magical term, an open sesame to the Third World soul. Events like India sending peace troops to the Korean war, Nehru shaking hands with the Yugoslav president, Josip Tito, were moments of pride. I cut these pictures out.

I also felt the bond between Nehru and Raj Kapoor. In fact, I felt Raj Kapoor's strange Chaplinesque socialism was Nehru simplified. I felt that his song in *Shree 420*, '*Mera joota hai Japani, yeh patloon Inglistani, Sar pe lal topi Roosi, phir bhi dil hai Hindustani*' was preferable to the national anthem. Decades later during the Perestroika[3] crisis, I visited Latvia and Estonia. My Finnish friends smuggled me in. I remember at one café the owner suddenly discovered we were Indians. He recited the

of which were newly independent, which took place on 18-24 April 1955 in Bandung, Indonesia. The conference's stated aims were to promote Afro-Asian economic and cultural cooperation and to oppose colonialism or neo-colonialism by any nation. The conference was an important step towards the Non-aligned Movement.

[3]Perestroika was a political movement for reformation within the Communist Party of the Soviet Union during the 1980s (1986), widely associated with Soviet leader Mikhail Gorbachev and his Glasnost (meaning 'openness') policy reform.

names Nehru and Raj Kapoor like open sesames of friendship. To add to it he said '*mein awara hoon*'. I realized this song had created a greater comradeship between India and Russia than any political slogan. Later during the Bhopal gas disaster[4] agitations I saw tribals who had come to express solidarity with the victims carry a huge shield of a tribal icon. It was a drawing of Stalin in huge soup-strainer moustaches and I realized the conversation had flown deeply both ways.

To my eyes, Nehru always appeared gentle but I liked the way his political Jeeves, V.K. Krishna Menon, he-of-the-hooked-nose, could pour acid on India's behalf. I remember Menon telling some hapless foreigner, 'Don't tell me about English, you merely picked it up, but I learned it.' I oozed with a nationalist pride sensing even then that spectators feel more strongly about the nation than its actual leaders. When my father let slip that Krishna Menon and Allen Lane were the co-founders of the legendary Penguin Books, my sense of literature was complete. Later when Octavio Paz and Pablo Neruda became ambassadors to India, I felt we

---

[4]The Bhopal disaster, also referred to as the Bhopal gas tragedy, was a gas leak incident in India, considered the world's worst industrial disaster. It occurred on the night of 2-3 December 1984 at the Union Carbide India Limited (UCIL) pesticide plant in Bhopal, Madhya Pradesh. Over 500,000 people were exposed to methyl isocyanate (MIC) gas and other chemicals. The toxic substance made its way into and around the shanty towns located near the plant. Estimates vary on the death toll. The official immediate death toll was 2,259. The government of Madhya Pradesh confirmed a total of 3,787 deaths. Others estimate that 8,000 died within two weeks, and another 8,000 or more have since died from gas-related diseases.

were truly international. Delhi, not New York, was the cosmopolitan centre of the world. The fact that I had never travelled further than Calcutta did not matter. My Delhi was a figment of a child's world. I wish it had remained that way.

I came from a family where there were many scientists. Many of them would come home and talk to my father. Talking science meant talking Nehru as he was an enthusiast for science. Science was something international and Pugwash[5] to me was an Indian idea. Nehru invited Bertrand Russell and Albert Einstein to hold a conference in 1955 but Cyrus Eaton, the Canadian-American investment banker and one of the most powerful financiers of the American Midwest, hijacked it. For me science and peace went hand in hand in the Nehruvian years. Between my childhood heroes, Linus Pauling, Russell and Nehru, peace was around the corner. In fact, to me Einstein felt like a Gandhi with a PhD degree. I shared my father's sense of internationalism, a Nehruvian vintage that I still carry years later. In those moments, the India of Nehru made us feel cosmopolitan and international, ready to embrace the world. Our socialism smelt of justice and other futuristic ideals and was still not tainted by the desperation of the ration card and other rituals of waiting.

---

[5]The Pugwash Conferences on Science and World Affairs is an international organization that brings together scholars and public figures to work towards reducing the danger of armed conflict and to seek solutions to global security threats. It was founded in 1957 by Joseph Rotblat and Bertrand Russell in Pugwash, Nova Scotia, Canada, following the release of the Russell-Einstein Manifesto in 1955.

Politics gave childhood a utopian quality which was magical. The magic wand of that era was truly political. It opened up worlds and also kept worlds open.

Central to an understanding of Nehru had to be the sheer visuality of the man. He was an aesthetic delight with his Nehru cap and his Nehru jacket. He was semiotically a perfect foil, a contrast to Gandhi. Gandhi embodied the fragility and power of the body, something that prompted the imperial Winston Churchill to call him the naked fakir. Gandhi himself realized the politics involved in the body and dress. After meeting the British monarch, King George V, he claimed that the king 'had enough clothes for both of us'. Gandhi was the archetypal peasant and Nehru, the immaculate aristocrat. If Gandhi reflected the truth of the satyagrahi, Nehru embodied the privileges of an aristocracy. Clothes were critical. They were statements of a culture, a message about biculturalism. When one looks at photographs of Nehru one senses he was literally modelling for India. He was the great Indian idol/ideal. He could make a Churchill or a Lord Mountbatten feel clumsy. Imperial upmanship was helpless against the aesthetic impact of the man. As Gandhi and Nehru stood together, a child felt that the worlds of civilization and nation, town and country, religious and secular were completely bridged. They represented the alchemy, the magic of the new Indian whole. Gandhi's khadi was rudimentary, a statement of need. Nehru's kurta was an aristocratic statement of the twinning of the ascetic and the aesthetic. They were two immaculate conceptions embodying two notions of the body politic. With them, one felt India had a semiotic answer to the dualisms of the world. The complementarity between the two was profound.

*

I must confess my nationalism ended with childhood. It was a period when nationalism felt different, more innocent, more unexpected. It was more a formula for surprise and emergence than a theory of predictability. It was a bit like my mother's idlis, immaculate in their whiteness, alive to the possibility of podi, chutney, sambhar or thokku. It combined unity and diversity. Nationalism was a form of hospitality, an openness to the world. I was utterly proud that Nehru invited the Dalai Lama and the Tibetans to settle in India. I felt they were not refugees but people coming home to India. Tibetans and the Dalai Lama added a grace, another possibility to the idea of nation in India. For me, it was obvious that Mother Teresa should come to India. Both Mother Teresa and the Dalai Lama made my India more complete. I remember the scientist John Burdon Sanderson Haldane (JBS) came to settle in India in 1956 after the Suez crisis and I felt India would be peppered with such exemplars. My father felt JBS was already an Indian who accidentally lived in England. His work on diversity felt almost Hindu. Nationalism for me was not a part of history. As a child it was part of the folklore, of the experimentation which Nehru's reputation, and his presence, made possible. My nationalism did not need a puritan sense of history. It was an Arabian Nights' tale of story-telling where

India became a storehouse of possibilities. There was an intellectual confidence to it anchored in my father's conviction that the arrogance of Churchill's cigar would fizzle out before the hum of Gandhi's charkha. Nationalism for him was an antidote to race, an answer to the injustices of colonialism. It was not really needed after Independence. It was a heuristic, a scaffolding for the emergence of the nation-state.

What gave me, my father and Nehru that confidence was our faith in science. Science in the Nehruvian era was not an act of faith or a dogma but a way of life. What marked it was the openness of the experiment. The experiment as a narrative banned closure and dogma. To experiment was to affirm life and its unexpectedness. To be part of the Nehruvian experiment was to be part of the future. Science was a wonderful, amiable way of walking into the future.

I felt terms like development, secularism, science, history, all were experiments, open works subject to further exploration. Science was play for Nehru. In the initial years of Independence, Nehru would rush over to NPL (National Physical Laboratory) in the capital, to talk science with K.S. Krishnan, the first director. There was a sense that science was play, an extension of childhood into the realms of knowledge. This sense of science as culture, as part of a future aesthetics was central to the Indian imagination. One witnessed it in the great array of Nehruvian scientists. One thinks of Homi Bhabha, P.C. Mahalanobis, Hussain Zaheer, K.S. Krishnan, Satish Dhawan and A. Rahman. Each brought a sense of beauty to the science they did. In fact, for many, the idea of import substitution was a puritanical dismal idea of science, a way of curbing dreams and turning science into pure instrumentality. These men wanted to create a culture for science not to improve GNP (Gross National Product) but to create a world where science as an imagination dreamt of a different world. The idea of transfer of technology was seen as a dismal science. When one thinks of ISI (Indian Statistical Institute), PRL (Physical Research Laboratory), TITR (Telecommunication and Information Technology Research Institute), the IITs (Indian Institutes of Technology), NID (National Institute of Design), one thinks of science as an aesthetic way of weaving knowledge. It is interesting that all these aesthetic centres of pilgrimage in science were built in the Nehruvian era. There was confidence of a different kind, what one of the later critics, Atma Ram, called a race for the Olympic medals of science, a dream of contributing breakthroughs to knowledge. We wanted to make sense to the world.

*

I admit there was an innocence to this world, where Gandhi was in heaven and Nehru in Delhi, which created an 'all's right with the world' feeling. It was not just the innocence of my childhood. Nehru himself had the touch of innocence. In later years, when I was researching for a book on corruption, I read that the Indian Institute of Public Administration (IIPA) had been established by Nehru on the basis of the Paul

Appleby Report. The Maxwell school professor argued that India was among the ten most honest nations of the world. Jawaharlal Nehru loved the Appleby Report and recommended it to his ministers, convinced that Appleby was right. In his assessment, there was a simplicity to the world, whereas the engineer, scholar and statesman, and the former Diwan of Mysore, Sir Mokshagundam Visvesvaraya, believed character-building, dam-building and nation-building went together. Sometimes I see that world as a kaleidoscopic world, a world full of unexpected colour. As the magic died, we subjected it to the scrutiny of the lens. Story-telling gave way to social science. When I think back on it, I see it as a piece of sculpture, a painting, even a large landscape and I watch it with awe and nostalgia. It looks beautiful and it had integrity. Discount it any way you want. The lines were clean, the strokes exuded imagination and integrity. Design, plan, science, nation-building all evoked a sense of beauty, the playful imagination of a new world being invented.

It was embodied in our pride in Corbusier's Chandigarh.Chandigarh was a symbolic answer to Partition. We needed an aesthetic answer to genocide and the Swiss-French architect, genius that he was, created one in Chandigarh. The fact that it was not organic was secondary. Corbusier in India was a claim to the future we all desperately wanted. My father summed it up towards the end. He said we were innocent, we were idealistic and we could afford to be. Our world worked and our dream came true. He would laugh at the Modi regime today, at its self-description as aspirational. For him, his era had the dreams, more ideals came true, more lives changed. He added that today a Nehruvian world may not be possible. Innocence, he felt, needed an ecology to survive. Later he added that the Nehruvian era was like vintage hockey. Indians were the originals. He talked of the 1936 Olympics where India played the USA. We began with shoes and found we were not used to them. Then we took them off and thrashed USA 21-0. The West knew how to undermine us. It changed the rules of the game, brought in Astroturf, synthetic carpeting designed to look like grass. Few Indians had seen anything like it. Nehru, like Indian hockey, could not adapt to the new rules of the game.

I realize as one who lived through the Nehruvian world, one needs the honesty to talk of the greying of this world. For me the end of childhood came in two quick strokes. India lost the war to China and India lost the Olympics in Rome to Pakistan. It was not victory that mattered, it was the despair that followed it. After the China war, we asked a new set of questions about science. Science was disconnected from play and culture, it was no more the gift of free knowledge which the noted physicist K.S. Krishnan, his mentor, Nobel Laureate C.V. Raman, or even a Subrahmanyan Chandrasekhar,[6] celebrated. Science was now a dismal science as we hooked it to technology. Science was now instrumental, it was applied science. It was as if

---

[6]Indian American astrophysicist who was awarded the Nobel Prize for Physics along with William A. Fowler in 1983.

the accountant had dismissed the poets and taken over a strange word called policy. Our cultural confidence took a beating. We now wanted nuclear bombs to shore up our importance, we wanted to score high in GNP ratings, we were desperate for the world to acclaim us. We realized we were no longer original and felt we belonged to the second-rate and second rank. In fact, we secretly felt a third-rate science was adequate for a Third World people.

A military defeat puts us into cultural panic. We questioned the entire paradigm, our science, our technology, our army, our foreign policy. Aesthetically, even Nehru shrank before our eyes, looking like a frail man, whose dreams had died on him. Nehru died in 1964. The very question rampant at that time, 'After Nehru, who?' expressed the sadness of an end of an era. The next twenty years saw the fading of that ideal. What transformed the Nehruvian possibility was the Emergency, a period of dictatorship where every Nehruvian institution disappeared.

*

When a culture collapses, its sense of goodness, of beauty, its code of ethics weakens. Worse, the very people we thought of as Nehruvian destroyed Nehru. All it needed was Indira Gandhi's desperation for power and Sanjay Gandhi's sense of illiteracy and evil to make a caricature of the Nehruvian space. The Emergency was a strange surreal inversion of categories. Planning, which was supposed to battle poverty, now sought to eliminate the poor. Family planning violated every rule of the body politic to sterilize our people.

Sanjay's behaviour showed he had no sense of Nehruvian values. Nehru celebrated the power of the word. He loved language. For Sanjay a word was not a word but a tool, preferably a cheap hammer. His sense of a message was a diktat or a telegram, while Nehruvians wallowed in epics and novels. The decline of language was central to the Emergency. Censorship came later. His cryptic words 'work more, talk less' summed up the spirit of the Emergency era where silence, fear and backroom gossip substituted for open creativity. Suddenly the middle class loved tyranny. Order acquired a power over dissent and difference and the Nehruvian way of life seemed brittle.

When language declines and life becomes instrumental, evil enters in a different way, easily subverting the ethical and the aesthetic. Politics loses out to the bureaucratic and every act of evil is now banalized as a production statistic or a clerical quota. I remember the Shâh Commission reporting about an old man well into his seventies, murmuring he was incapable of the sexual act, still being sterilized to fulfil a quota. We discarded parliamentary democracy for the world where Sanjay was the God, Stalin and Catechism of the Emergency. It was a slapstick world which made no sense and yet people praised it, making it more absurd. My father hated him but more because he thought Sanjay's incompetence and illiteracy bordered on the evil. I remember the day he told us that he had been to the defence laboratory where they were testing the

Maruti car. It ran a distance of forty-five miles before the doors fell apart. My father was sure the Emergency would also fall apart in a similar way.

But evil is more than a mechanical problem. Sanjay and Indira destroyed the ecology of democracy but what surprised many was that there was little resistance from the Nehruvians. The intellectual world of science and journalism sang Sanjay's praises and echoed his call for discipline in a celebration of autism never seen before, as when Dev Kant Barooah, the then president of the Indian National Congress, exclaimed in his one effort at poetry that Indira was India and India was Indira. It was a crudity Nehru would not have imagined.

For the generation of the 1950s, Nehruvianism was a lived world. Its assumptions were taken for granted, often inarticulate in their tacitness. When asked what Nehru embodied, people in my class would refer to a plan or a project, point to Chandigarh, talk of TIFR (Tata Institute of Fundamental Research) or refer to Panchsheel or the Five Year Plan. Few articulated its axiomatic values. This taken-for-grantedness proved fragile. When people violated Nehru's ideas in the name of Nehru, one watched silently. From a public space or a commons, Nehruvianism became a privileged world, a legacy of many families. It was a retreat that weakened democracy. It showed that Nehruvian as an idea ceased being inventive. All the creativity belonged to the first decade. All the great institutions were built then. The later eras became a nostalgia rather than an inventive process. As a result, the Congress could bowdlerize Nehru, and Indira Gandhi, like a tyrannical

Alice could insist that words meant what she said they meant. By the Emergency, Nehruvian ideas could not function even as Linus' blanket.[7] After the Emergency, they were abandoned by the state. They drifted into civil society, and into dissenting imaginations. As many old Nehruvians challenged the dams, one felt the life of the idea had run a full cycle.

Despite the Partition and the Bengal Famine, despite the atom bomb, the Nehruvian world lacked a sense of evil. Part of the reason lay in the language of progressiveness and social engineering. Many felt that with the right values and the right technology, any problem was solvable. Maybe science and socialism as a science secularized evil so that when evil emerged from the roots of the family itself, we watched helplessly. Looking back, I cannot think of a major book on the end of the Nehru era which has the complexity of a novel. There are letters, diaries, autobiographies, commissions' reports like the records of the Shah Commission but there was no major study which was like a Dostoevskian probe into the roots of the Emergency. Protest there was but protest hardly crystallizes into analysis.

When evil is not met head-on, it survives, and seeps into the crevices of society. It begins banalizing ideas. The tragedy of the later era was to watch Nehruvianism turn second-rate and this too was a family effort. The banalization of Nehru was, I think, the final consequence of the Emergency. When evil becomes piecemeal,

[7]A character in the popular *Peanuts* comic strip, who is almost never without his blue security blanket.

monotonous, everyday, we begin accepting it as the norm.

After Bangladesh, there was little that was Nehruvian about India. By the time of Rajiv, Sonia and Rahul, the ideas of Nehru constituted a form of autism.

In an odd way, there is little of Nehru in memory. I confess there is a lot of Nehru in folklore, in the oral tradition, in the tacitness of a generation's lives, but little of it is text and less is a part of the literacy of the next generation. The imagination of the Nehruvian world did not emerge.

Let me borrow two terms from the novelist and critic U.R. Ananthamurthy. He claimed that Indian culture is very much like a house, with a front yard and a backyard. The front yard is official, formal, even legalistic. The backyard, beginning with the kitchen, was backstage. It was informal, feminine, the place for story-telling. Deep down, the Nehruvian imagination had no backyard. There was always something official about it. Ironically, the Nehruvian world was a failure of story-telling, lacking anecdotes of doubt. It was a bit like the silence of Partition. The pain of the refugee, the stories of rape, went underground while a progressive generation talked about Nilokheri[8] and community development and transfer of power. In some

[8]Established in 1948 by the social visionary S.K. Dey, at Karnal in Punjab (now Haryana), as a new township to house displaced families after Partition, Nilokheri was planned as the capital of the new state of Punjab. Jawaharlal Nehru called it the town of his dreams. But heavy floods threatened its development, and Chandigarh became the capital of Punjab.

ways, Nehruvianism was incomplete as a sensorium. It was powerful visually, it was impressive in terms of the monumentality of sight. Yet, it discouraged doubt and listening. If it had been also a culture of the ear, of the backyard, it might have been less brittle and created its own vitality of doubt as part of its paradigm.

That was its final irony. Today as one watches Narendra Modi and Rahul Gandhi create a 'Nehru mukt Bharat', as I watch a new generation treat secularism, planning and socialism as dirty words, I realize the desperate need to understand the Nehruvian experiment. It was not about the failure of plans, or the decline of institutions, it was in a deep way the growing mediocrity of an idea. The challenge today is to invent it differently, to create a heuristics and poetics of the world as a new probe into the future. We need a new tryst with destiny as a new way of story-telling. Sadly our shamans are missing.

Nehru: The Homemaker

Rakesh Batabyal

In August 1947, when Jawaharlal Nehru was in the process of forming his Cabinet, he wrote to Sardar Vallabhbhai Patel, his comrade of several years, that adhering to the formalities that needed to be observed to some extent, he was writing to ask Patel 'to join the new Cabinet'.[1] 'This writing', Nehru, added, was 'somewhat superfluous' because the Sardar to him was 'the strongest pillar of the Cabinet'.[2] Patel responded with equal warmth, in words that had a touch of both greatness and gratitude:

> Our attachment and affection for each other and our comradeship for an unbroken period of nearly thirty years admit of no formalities. My services will be at your disposal, I hope for the rest of my life, and you will have unquestioned loyalty and devotion from me in the cause for

[1]Jawaharlal Nehru to Vallabhbhai Patel, 3 August 1947, *Selected Correspondence of Sardar Patel*, p.537.

[2]*Ibid.*

> which no man in India has sacrificed as much as you have done. Our combination is unbreakable and therein lies our strength. I thank you for the sentiments expressed in your letter.[3]

This correspondence between the two men—who are now painted in some political circles as ideological opponents, even adversaries—is glorious proof that the struggle against the colonial power had fostered a unique sense of solidarity and mutual respect among the leaders of the freedom movement and the people who supported and admired them. The national movement and the space that it opened up created hundreds of such relationships.[4] The space that Nehru, Patel and several other leaders shared was like home.

A home is a web of intricate relationships binding friends, family and kin. It is a place where one is generally secure both from external danger and internal uncertainties. However, making a home, and guarding it—sometimes from itself—is a tough and torturous job. It may be an interesting idea to see Nehru, India's first prime minister, as a 'homemaker'—an 'accommodator', a consensus builder; a leader who tried to organize the incipient nation as a home, with the aim of providing succour, stability and a sense of future to all its residents.

The leaders of the Indian national movement, particularly from the 1920s, were already engaged in

---

[3]Vallabhbhai, Patel to Jawaharlal Nehru, *ibid*.

[4]Visalakshi Menon, *Indian Women and Nationalism: The U.P. Story*, Haranand, 2004; Aparna Basu, *Mridula Sarabhai: Rebel with a Cause*, OUP, Delhi,1996.

creating such an expansive idea of the home. A large number of women could, for example, occupy the public sphere in unprecedented ways. The national movement had affected and altered the nature of the public sphere and the engagement of the private with it. A completely different understanding of the family could be seen in the Sabarmati Ashram or at Wardha, and still more different were the relationships that grew among freedom movement activists in the prisons.[5] The idea of home and family now extended beyond traditional filial relationships; it was a new kinship, born out of a shared mass struggle.

*

Nehru, unlike many of his contemporaries, had come to the Indian National Congress because of his family's association with the party and the ongoing nationalist movement. To every member of the large Nehru clan, Swaraj Bhavan in Allahabad was family.[6] Jawaharlal grew up in this bustling, dynamic space and had to evolve his own relationships with his many kin. In later years Nehru exhibited a strong sense of family and concern for its well-being. Very rarely did a member of the family suffer his neglect—though he was himself always conscious of the effect that his long absences and his preoccupation with the national movement had on his wife Kamala

[5]Visalakshi Menon, *op. cit.*

[6]See Krishna Nehru Hutheesing, *We Nehrus*, Pearl Publications Private Limited, Bombay, 1967.

and daughter Indira. He tried, very consciously, to make up for this by spending as much time as he could with Kamala during the years when she was seriously ill, and by writing Indira long and frequent letters from prison.

His immediate relationships, however, did not exhaust Nehru's idea of a family. Many of his friends were part of the extended home: Rafi Ahmed Kidwai, Subhas Bose, Jayaprakash Narayan (JP), Krishna Menon, Ram Manohar Lohia and many others. Relations with some of them were sometimes delicate, and sometimes turned difficult, but Nehru rarely broke with them of his own. Nowhere was this more noticeable than in his relationships with Gandhi, Bose and Patel within the Congress. He remained cordial even with Lohia and JP, though they became his greatest critics.

Nehru critiqued Gandhi's worldview in many fundamental ways but he was in complete agreement with Gandhi's methods of struggle, which was the basis of their close and enduring relationship. On the other hand, Subhas Bose was a comrade despite the fact that Nehru was emphatic in his rejection of the former's endorsement of violent struggle and his too-pragmatic approach during the Second World War, which led him to seek the support of the Nazi and Japanese military regimes to rid India of British rule. However—and this is a significant fact that is almost never emphasized—when Bose entered into a no-win battle with Gandhi in 1939-40, Nehru tried till the end to mediate and pacify both sides so that there could be a reconciliation.

This preference for reconciliation and

accommodation—indeed, kinship—was even more apparent in Nehru's relationship with Sardar Patel, especially immediately after Independence. Many of Nehru's detractors and admirers have maintained that there was a kind of rivalry between the two, that relations between them were strained and each man tried to undermine the other. After all, both men articulated their disagreements in private and public communications. But this is a simplistic understanding of the nature of their relationship. The differences, and sometimes serious disagreements, were always only on issues of governance;[7] the two leaders remained comrades in the project of nation-building, and their respect and affection for each other remained intact.

One of the earliest instances of disagreement between them was when Nehru, as prime minister, sent his secretary, a senior civil servant, to Ajmer where a communal riot had broken out in late 1947.[8] Patel, who was home minister and deputy prime minister, found this inappropriate. He felt that this not only humiliated the local chief commissioner but also amounted to tinkering with the established processes of administration. Nehru, however, thought that what he had done was to send a strong message, which was important at the time, and that it did not violate any code of propriety.

[7]See Jawaharlal Nehru to Vallabhbhai Patel, 20 February 1950, Durga Das, ed., *Sardar Patel's Correspondence, 1945-50*, Vol. 10, pp.1-5; 26 March 1950, *ibid.*, pp.9-14.

[8]Vallabhbhai Patel to Jawaharlal Nehru, *ibid.*, Vol. 6, 8-9; Vallabhbhai Patel to H.V.R Iengar, Principal Secretary to the Prime Minister, 23 December 1947.

Nehru saw his intervention as a sign of reassurance to his countrymen and also to the world about the intent of the new government. Administration, in his understanding, also needed to carry a political message.[9] But Patel believed that the majesty of the state, which operated in this case through the bureaucracy, was enough to sustain the broader vision of the Constitution and the government.

The roots of this disagreement lay in very different ideas about prime ministership in the new nation. For Patel, the prime minister was one among equals, different only in the fact that he provided moral guidance to his team and the nation. (In this, he was transporting the nature of the Congress leadership onto the functioning of the government.) Nehru, on the other hand, believed that the prime minister's position was not that of *primus inter pares*, and that he could act independent of the Cabinet. The issue brought both of them to Gandhi through separate notes and both wanted to relinquish their governmental position if Gandhi agreed.[10] Communication reflecting disagreement between Patel and Nehru on this, as on other matters, was frank, and points to the still fluid nature of the Cabinet system in the country. Nehru wrote to Patel that he was 'hurt by

---

[9]Jawaharlal Nehru to Vallabhbhai Patel, 23 December 1947, *ibid.*, pp.10-11.

[10]'Mr. Nehru's note of 6 January 1948 to Mahatma Gandhi' enclosed in Jawaharlal Nehru to Vallabhbhai Patel, 11 January, 1948, *ibid.*, Vol. 6, pp.17-21; see also Vallabhbhai Patel's 'Note to Mahatma Gandhi', enclosed in Vallabhbhai Patel to Jawaharlal Nehru, 12 January 1948, *ibid.*, pp.21-24.

the references of Sardar's disagreements over many of Nehru's policies'.[11] Sardar's response brought out, again, the depth of the camaraderie between these captains of the freedom struggle. He wrote, on 28 March 1950:

> Both age and health have conspired to cheat me of the full enjoyment and pleasure of carrying the heavy burden I have been undertaking in the cause of the country. If I have persisted, it has been only with a desire to strengthen your hands, share your burden and continue to serve the country in the evening of my life. I have also held to the position because I have felt that our joint efforts are essential to pull the country though one crisis after another which have unfortunately affected the course of its history after Partition.[12]

Mahatma Gandhi's assassination—which was a great blow to both—brought to the fore another area of difference between Nehru and Patel. The Mahatma's assassin, Nathuram Godse, had been associated with the Rashtriya Swayamsevak Sangh (RSS) and the Hindu Mahasabha (HMS), Hindu supremacist organizations that now came under scrutiny. Though Sardar Patel was convinced of the communal nature of the RSS, he saw the Hindu Mahasabha as the bigger danger

---

[11]A good discussion on the issue has been in James Manor, ed., *Nehru to the Ninete is The Changing Office of the Prime Minister in India,* Viking Publishers, Delhi, 1994.

[12]Vallabhbhai Patel to Jawaharlal Nehru, 28 March 1950, *ibid.*, p.21.

to the country.[13] He believed that the latter, being a political organization—unlike the former, which was a socio-cultural organization—had greater power to inflict damage to communal amity. The fact that in 1948-49 he was satisfied with the RSS's promise of keeping away from politics while earlier, in 1945-46, he had resolved to finish off the Mahasabha electorally testifies to this understanding. The RSS did, of course, go on to create other political outfits once the Hindu Mahasabha could no longer serve its purpose, but Patel did not live long enough to see that he was mistaken in his assessment.

Unlike Patel, Nehru never had any illusions about the RSS. He had long held that communalism was the biggest danger to Indian society, and he knew that the RSS was the ideological spring of Hindu communal ideology that created and sustained the Hindu Mahasabha and similar outfits. Hence, he was very clear that the RSS should not be allowed to occupy public space.

Notwithstanding these differences, communication between Nehru and Patel was open enough and their commitment to the common goal of nation-building remained intact. Unwilling to let things reach breaking point, both even offered to leave the government. When Patel died in 1950, Nehru confessed that he would now have to plough on alone: '[I] will feel rather forlorn and certain emptiness will steal upon me', he said in

---

[13]Vallabhbhai Patel to Syama Prasad Mukherjee, 18 July 1948, *ibid.*, pp.321-22; Vallabhbhai Patel to Jawaharlal Nehru, 4 May 1948, *ibid.*, p.320.

Parliament.[14] After the Mahatma's death, Nehru had expressed his sense of loneliness to Rajendra Prasad. Now, without Patel, his old comrade, that sense was even keener, especially as close friends of the past, like Rafi Ahmed Kidwai, were embroiled in politics in the states and were becoming more trouble than troubleshooters. The sense of 'home' was diminishing.

*

This sense of loneliness was aggravated by Nehru's increasing realization that the party, the Indian National Congress, which was his family in more senses than one, was getting isolated—both from its own ideological universe as well as from popular sympathy in a large and populous, newly independent nation. This may well have been an exaggerated feeling of things changing, or coming undone, as Nehru was besieged by complaints from different Congressmen. Adding to the party's and the government's difficulties in governance were Britain's manoeuvres to deny India its pound sterling balance and to complicate the quick settlement of the very straightforward issue of the 1947 external aggression in Kashmir.[15]

And yet, Nehru was clear that India would be part of the Commonwealth family. This he did despite the risk of losing popular support, given the resentment over

[14]Jawaharlal Nehru, Speech in Parliament, 15 December 1950.

[15]Chandrasekhar Dasgupta, *War and Diplomacy in Kashmir*, 1947-48, New Delhi, 2002.

the stance Britain had adopted on the pound sterling and Kashmir issues. Besides, there could have been a groundswell of emotions against such a move just after Independence.

There was another complication that could have made Nehru turn away from the Commonwealth project. Fearing further disintegration of its empire and areas of influence, Britain tried to create an anti-communist flank by roping in the some Commonwealth countries in 1950 at the Colombo Conference.[16] India at this time was facing a communist rebellion in Telangana and an aggressive Communist Party—which had in 1948 declared the Congress government as the government of the comprador bourgeoisies. Yet, Nehru was determined not to allow Britain and the United States to use 'the communist menace' as a ruse to suppress many independence and anti-colonialism movements in Africa and Asia. Instead of walking away, in an act of solidarity, he played a leading role at the Colombo Conference to force a shift in the Commonwealth position.

*

Through all this, for a 'homemaker', the arrival of millions of refugees from East and West Pakistan was an issue to be tackled diligently. Not only was rehabilitation a challenge, there was also the danger of widespread

[16]Rakesh Batabyal, 'The Imperial Embers and the Invocation to Cold War: Colombo Conference 1950', Proceedings of the Indian History Congress, Vol. 74, 2013.

violence. In the highly charged atmosphere, with news and rumours coming in about targeted killings across the new borders, there were political and ostensibly cultural organizations ready to exploit the situation to suit their communal agenda. The Congress had been trying to fight communal ideology for over three decades leading up to Independence but had found it hard to counter Muslim communalism. Now it was face to face with the potential might of Hindu communal forces. For Nehru, religious harmony was an article of faith. Ever vigilant, he had expressed his anger when, in late 1949, a statue of Ram was secretly installed in the mosque at Ayodhya. Warning that it could have grave consequences for India's future, he had urged and directed his fellow Congressman, Govind Ballabh Pant, who was then chief minister of the United Provinces, to take corrective action. But the idol remained, as the local administration refused to remove it, citing a threat to public peace. Nehru was to later publicly admit that the event had shamed him.

The next time he saw a similar danger to the future of India's democracy and secular character, Nehru acted with greater resolve. In 1950, a senior Congressman, Purushottam Das Tandon, stood for election to the party's presidency. Nehru had, for some time, been quite concerned about Tandon's ideological orientations. Tandon had played a key role in the vociferous campaign to make Hindi the official language in the Constitution, as against the argument by many like Nehru who wanted Hindustani, which was more representative of a very large section of Indian society. Earlier, Tandon had disagreed with Nehru's conviction that how Pakistan treated its Hindu minority population could in no way determine India's attitude towards its own minorities, especially Indian Muslims. He had also aligned himself with outfits that championed Hindu communal and revivalist issues.

In a bitterly fought election, Purushottam Das Tandon won the presidency of the Congress. To Nehru, having as president someone who held and articulated views which were at variance with the ideals of the party was not at all a welcome proposition.[17] Writing to B.C. Roy he declared that he was readying to fight it out: it would either be Tandon's line or his that would hold in the Congress.[18] For him the party was his own home as well as the chief instrument with which to make the larger home, i.e., a democratic, secular and inclusive independent India. Through the party, and as prime minister, therefore, he was trying to give certain broad directions, certain approaches to fulfil long cherished goals: that, like the party, India would be for the underdog, and that it would be non-communal.[19] The aim was not only to remove barriers to development, but also to create a society of equal citizens.[20] To allow any deviation from these core

[17]Jawaharlal Nehru to P.D. Tandon, 30 March 1951, S. Gopal, ed., *Selected Works of Jawaharlal Nehru.*

[18]Jawaharlal Nehru to B.C. Roy, 17 August 1951, *ibid.*

[19]*Ibid.*, Vol. 16, p.162.

[20]Presidential Address, *Ibid.*, p.210.

principles within the Congress was to allow a weakening of the 'inner fibres of this great organization'.[21]

It was clear to Nehru that 'ideas and persons foreign to [the party] in the past' had come in.[22] Like a surgeon, therefore, he would work to excise them. He announced: There should be no role for reactionaries here.[23] It was part of an integrated view, what party workers thought 'of the Congress, of our own country or of the world'.[24] The Congress to him needed to be seen in terms of a party working for an equitable society and for world peace.[25] One of the basic planks of this was communal unity, on which the Congress stood.[26] Secularism as a philosophy was integral to the party and the country.

Perhaps Nehru felt the need to be particularly forceful about this because his comrade Sardar Patel, though obviously anti-communal himself, did not articulate this view often enough in very clear-cut ideological terms. Many a time his approach to matters was so nuanced as to lead to contrary interpretations. He went strictly by the constitutional arrangements for the minorities in the future republic. Nehru on the other hand was not entirely enchanted with the constitutional

[21] *Ibid.*

[22] *Ibid.*

[23] *Ibid.* p.222.

[24] *Ibid.* p.211.

[25] The basic ideals of the Congress, 1951, *ibid.*, Vol. 15, p.113.

[26] *Ibid.*, p.114.

pronouncements and guarantees; he wanted to ensure that the character of the state itself was an advertisement of the secular principle. His secular India would do more than merely follow, mechanically, the Constitution in letter; it would provide the security and warmth of a home to its minorities. And in this the Congress Party had a central role to play.

Thus, a new party president having a vision contrary to this was unacceptable to Nehru. The Congress Party, with all its members, was his family, but he could also not allow it to be completely uprooted from its ideological soil.[27] He could not allow such a capture of his 'home'. He would soon launch a bristling attack and by 1951 he would install himself as the president of the Congress so as to preempt any other fundamental ideological shift.

*

In a country where an overwhelming majority made a living—often barely—as farmers or agricultural labour, any effort to settle the home would have been incomplete without bringing about change in the villages. India's vast peasantry lived a life of exploitation, squalor and inertia in 558,000 scattered settlements. According to the census of 1951, 96 percent of India's population of 357 million lived in villages, and 82.7 percent belonged to the

[27]Nehru Urges Congress to Adhere to Basic Ideals, Presidential Speech at 57th session of the Congress, *The Times of India*, Delhi, 19 October 1951.

agricultural classes.[28] Any talk of a modern society, and that too a socialist society, required a radical change in the lives of this vast segment of the Indian population.

Nehru's politics had begun by mobilizing the peasants in the United Province in the early 1930s. (This had earned him the ire of the landlords, most of whom also constituted the core of the Muslim League, which was a main reason for the League's anti-Nehru stand.[29]) Today, most analysts remember him as the main architect of national planning, which, it has been argued, has developed a technocratic, urban-based system of planning. But a closer look will provide a different picture. The village was central to Nehru's overall vision.

Nehru, trained as he was in the scientific tradition, wanted concrete institutions to take control of the issue at hand. It was here that he saw the Community Development Programme as the ideal tool, for it could help develop institutions required to intervene at the village level, while at the same time ensuring popular participation in decision-making, a *sine qua non* for Nehru's vision of inclusive democracy. He was no

---

[28]S.C. Dube, *India's Changing Villages: Human Factors in Community Development*, Allied Publishers, Bombay, 1958, p.7.

[29]In fact many of those who take a softer intellectual stand on the Muslim League or defend its communal position end up taking a very interestingly anti-Nehru stand even today. See for example, the position of Ayesha Jalal, *The Sole Spokesman: Jinnah, the Muslim League and the Demand for Pakistan*, Cambridge University Press, Cambridge, 1985, or even an anti-Nehru tirade by the British Marxist intellectual Perry Anderson, 'Why Partition', *London Review of Books*, Vol. 34, No. 14, 19 July 2012, pp.11-19.

votary of a romanticized village life, but he had seen in the early projects of community development in Itawa, Nilokheri and Faridabad a way to involve people in projects to improve their economic and socio-cultural condition. The connection between this and the general development of the country was very clear to him when he said in 1957:

> It is the peasant who has borne the burden of India in ages past. It is on the growth and betterment of our peasantry that the future of India must necessarily depend.[30]

The Congress ministries in many provinces had tried to bring in tenancy reforms, an area of governance extremely tricky to navigate given the power structure of Indian politics and society. Nehru led from the front in 1950 by forcing the Zamindari Abolition Act through a constitutional amendment when the zamindars in many places like Bihar filled the courts with cases. One of the biggest changes was the amalgamation of the princely states into the larger political administration. This and the first election of 1952 would make this structural change a permanent feature in the villages. This would, in its train, bring about deep changes in village life. A researcher in a remote Gujarat village, Kasandra, for example, wrote in 1950 that it was as 'a period of radical transformation in the village and [among] its inhabitants. The period of radical transformation had begun with Independence in 1947…among the major

[30]Jawaharlal Nehru, 'Salt of the Earth', September 1957, *Kurukshetra*, Government of India, Delhi, 1961.

reforms contemplated by the Congress Party was reform of the agrarian structure'.[31]

The first elections provided the political pathway to a changed rural landscape: the Village Level Workers (VLW) and National Extension Service (NES) took active national politics to the village level. Significantly, in doing their election studies, many field workers drew the insight that the changes in agrarian structure—through the abolition of the zamindari system, etc.—had fundamentally altered the nature of political participation as well as the nature of the polity in the villages for the better.[32]

Nehru, it was clear, saw the Community Development Programme as a means to entrench democracy in the villages. His idea of Panchayati Raj or democratic decentralization was intimately linked to his vision of such programmes anchoring institutions of local development. The old system was collapsing and the poor farm tenants, craftsmen and artisans now needed support from institutions in the new world. Capitalist penetration, to whatever extent it came, was not counterbalanced by any of the new systemic advantages. It was here that Nehru wanted the community development project to take the lead.[33]

---

[31]Gitel P. Steed, 'Notes on an Approach to a Study of Personality Formation in A Hindu Village in Gujarat', in Mckim Marriot, ed., *Village India*, Asia Publishing House, Bombay, 1961, pp.114-20.

[32]Anand Chakrabarti, 'A Village in Chomu Assembly Constituency in Rajasthan', in. M. Shah, ed., *The Grassroots of Democracy Field Studies of Indian Elections*, Permanent Black, Delhi, 2011, pp.31-45.

[33]A.R. Desai, 'Changing Profile of Rural Society in India', in A.R. Desai, ed., *Agrarian Struggles in India after Independence*, OUP, Bombay, 1986, p.22.

Different experiments in community development were being made in places like Itawa, Nilokheri, Faridabad and some areas in Tamil Nadu; the experiments had started almost immediately after Independence. Nehru now saw an expanded community development programme as the non-violent way of bringing revolutionary changes in village society at a time when in other countries, like China, such changes had violence attached to them.[34] It was one of Nehru's grandest projects, in many senses more ambitious than the project of erecting dams, factories and other such 'temples' of modernity.[35] Writing in the 1950s an astute social scientist, S.C. Dube, felt that the future of the entire subcontinent, and indeed of Asia, depended on the success of the Community Development Programme.[36]

By 1956-57 the recommendations of the Balvantray Mehta committee report on decentralization, commissioned by Nehru's government, had been introduced in Rajasthan. The entire political text of the Community Development Programme, as Nehru saw it, was clearly apparent in this beginning. It was a remarkable roadmap for a decentralized democracy—one where everyone, down to the village level, through the panchayats, would have ownership of the 'Idea of India', and India would be a large, open home to all its citizens.

---

[34]'Right to Live', *The Times of India*, Delhi, 14 May 1952, p.4.

[35]'Revolutionary Aim of the Community Work', *The Times of India*, Delhi, 20 April 1953, p.7.

[36]S.C. Dube, *op. cit.*, p.156.

This was the dream. What began to happen, however, was that increasing bureaucratization started to undermine the project. By the early 1960s it was difficult to find a trace of the original confident, self-reliant avatar of the Community Development Programme in the ministry-led and bureaucrat-controlled travesty that it had become. The village workers and the national extension service workers were spending more time filling forms than working the field. Nehru bemoaned the fact that the programme was in a rut.[37] The failure in this regard meant that Nehru's home-making efforts ended up promoting urban-led growth, something that he himself, having spent almost his entire political life for and among village folk, never wanted. This in turn created conditions for rural unrest in the future.[38] The failure of Nehru's grand project for genuine decentralization left India's numerous villages in filth and squalor, thereby pulling all of India's many success stories back to the meta-narrative of poverty and cultural degradation.

This tragic failure notwithstanding, Nehru as India's first prime minister needs to be celebrated as a visionary who created the institutional as well as ideological template for nation-building as a 'homemaking' process. The ideas and initiatives this inspired were of tremendous significance for the history of freedom and democracy of a large mass of humanity.

---

[37]'In the Rut', *The Times of India*, Delhi, 3 August 1963, p.6.

[38]A.R. Desai., ed., *Agrarian Struggles in India After Independence.*

and putting India on the developmental path starting from the abysmal initial conditions left behind by colonialism, which the Nobel Laureate Rabindranath Tagore had so evocatively expressed shortly before his death in 1941:[2]

> The wheels of fate will some day compel the English to give up their Indian Empire. What kind of India will they leave behind, what stark misery? When the stream of their centuries' administration runs dry at last, what a waste of mud and filth will they leave behind them.

At the time of Independence, India, with 84 percent illiteracy (92 percent among women), was a famine-ridden country with an average life expectancy of about thirty years (which meant the poor died much younger). Per capita income in India had been shrinking annually at 0.2 percent per annum for the previous three decades, agricultural output was shrinking at 0.72 percent per annum and food grains output was shrinking even faster at 1.14 percent per annum.[3] As we shall see below, Nehru was to launch a brilliant multi-pronged strategy to lift India out of this morass which set an example to numerous other countries emerging out of colonialism after the Second World War.

[2]Quoted in Bipan Chandra, Mridula Mukherjee, Aditya Mukherjee, *India Since Independence*, Penguin, New Delhi, 15th reprint 2014, p.13.

[3]See Aditya Mukherjee, 'The Return of The Colonial in Indian Economic History: The Last Phase of Colonialism in India', Presidential Address to the Indian History Congress (Modern India) in December 2007. (Reprinted in *Social Scientist*, Vol. 36, Nos. 3-4, March-April 2008.)

The Indian Economy in the Nehru Era

Aditya Mukherjee and
Mridula Mukherjee

In this essay we will attempt to assess Jawaharlal Nehru's contribution to the making of the post-colonial Indian economy. His contribution in this area was no less significant than his huge role in establishing and nurturing a secular and democratic polity in India, rescuing it from the mad holocaust-like situation created by the partition of the country and the murder of the Father of the Nation, Mahatma Gandhi, by Hindu communal forces who were hell-bent on using this opportunity to build a 'Hindu state', the counterpart of a 'Muslim' Pakistan.[1] In the economic sphere Nehru had the stupendous task of 'un-structuring' the colonial structuring of the Indian economy, which had occurred over two hundred years,

[1]See Mridula Mukherjee, 'Jawaharlal Nehru's Finest Hour: The Struggle for a Secular India', *Studies in People's History*, Vol. 1, No. 2, 2014 and 'Indian Democracy: Debt to Jawaharlal Nehru', *Mainstream*, Vol. 52, No. 23, 31 May 2014 for a fuller discussion of this aspect.

and putting India on the developmental path starting from the abysmal initial conditions left behind by colonialism, which the Nobel Laureate Rabindranath Tagore had so evocatively expressed shortly before his death in 1941:[2]

> The wheels of fate will some day compel the English to give up their Indian Empire. What kind of India will they leave behind, what stark misery? When the stream of their centuries' administration runs dry at last, what a waste of mud and filth will they leave behind them.

At the time of Independence, India with 84 percent illiteracy (92 percent among women), was a famine-ridden country with an average life expectancy of about thirty years (which meant the poor died much younger). Per capita income in India had been shrinking annually at 0.2 percent per annum for the previous three decades, agricultural output was shrinking at 0.72 percent per annum and food grains output was shrinking even faster at 1.14 percent per annum.[3] As we shall see below, Nehru was to launch a brilliant multi-pronged strategy to lift India out of this morass which set an example to numerous other countries emerging out of colonialism after the Second World War.

---

[2]Quoted in Bipan Chandra, Mridula Mukherjee, Aditya Mukherjee, *India Since Independence*, Penguin, New Delhi, 15th reprint 2014, p.23.

[3]See Aditya Mukherjee, 'The Return of The Colonial in Indian Economic History: The Last Phase of Colonialism in India', Presidential Address to the Indian History Congress (Modern India) in December 2007. (Reprinted in *Social Scientist*, Vol. 36, Nos. 3-4, March-April 2008.)

In recent years, however, there has been a growing tendency, particularly among neo-colonial scholars like Tirthankar Roy and Meghnad Desai, to dismiss or run down the economic achievements of the Nehruvian era. Looking back from the vantage point of the high growth rates since the economic reforms of 1991, the Nehru years are described as a wasted opportunity. The strategy of trying to reverse the colonial structuring of the Indian economy through inward-oriented, import-substituting self-reliant growth, which involved protecting the fledgling domestic industry, was seen as the main problem.[4] As Meghnad Desai put it, 'the first forty years of India's independence were wasted'.[5]

This assessment is completely ahistorical. If the post-1991 strategy was adopted in the 1950s India would surely have headed towards becoming a 'banana republic'. Conversely, it would not make any sense to apply the economic strategy of the 1950s in the 1990s when the nature of the global economy, including the Indian economy, had undergone fundamental changes. The Nehruvian era created the conditions for the future opening up and growth of the economy. Today's India is possible because of the base laid in the early decades after Independence and has not emerged despite it.

---

[4]See for example, Tirthankar Roy, 'Economic Legacies of Colonial Rule in India: Another Look', *Economic and Political Weekly*, Vol. 50, No. 15, 11 April 2015.

[5]Address at Bhoothalingam Centenary celebration, Nehru Memorial Museum and Library, New Delhi, 21 February 2009, organized by the National Council of Applied Economic Research. See also his *Rediscovery of India*, Bloomsbury, 2011.

Also, the Nehruvian phase has to be seen in the global historical context of that period. As former prime minister and economist Dr Manmohan Singh, who as finance minister inaugurated the structural adjustment programme for India in 1991, was to acknowledge: 'In 1960, if you had asked anybody which country would be on top of the league of the Third World in 1996 or 1997, India was considered to be the frontrunner.'[6] There was a consensus among a wide variety of economists in the world at that time, including among very prominent economists in the West—W.W. Rostow, Rosenstein-Rodan, Wilfred Malenbaum, George Rosen, Ian Little, Brian Reddaway, to name just a few—that the direction of the Indian planning effort was a very positive one with great potential. (It was common to eulogize the democratic Indian path as opposed to the model followed by 'totalitarian' China.) There was in fact a dialectical relationship between the evolution of contemporary development theory and the Indian experience. As the reputed economist Sukhamoy Chakravarty noted, 'Dominant ideas of contemporary development economics influenced the logic of India's plans, and correspondingly, development theory was for a while greatly influenced by the Indian case.'[7]

However, quite contrary to historical fact, the list of the alleged failures of Nehru in the economic sphere has kept growing: neglect of Indian agriculture,

[6] *Business Standard*, 9 January 1998.

[7] Sukhamoy Chakravarty, *Development Planning: The Indian Experience*, Clarendon Press, Oxford, 1987, pp.4, 81.

incomplete land reforms, neglect of primary education, over-emphasis on capital goods industries at the cost of consumer goods industries, statism and much else. The demonization of Nehru has received a definite impetus in recent years with the rise of the BJP (Bharatiya Janata Party), a political strand which was not only not linked with the national liberation movement which chalked out the 'Idea of India' but stood diametrically opposed to it. It is this 'Idea of India', which Nehru brilliantly tried to implement in the newly born independent Indian state, and the BJP naturally has no sympathy for it.

To students of contemporary history like us, this demonization of Nehru looks like the world upside down. In this essay we will make a brief attempt to set the record straight.[8]

The Parameters Bequeathed by the National Movement

The path that was followed after Independence to undertake the stupendous task of rebuilding the Indian economy, ravaged by colonialism, was not chosen by Nehru alone. The independent Indian state, which

[8]Some of the arguments made here were also presented by Aditya Mukherjee on the following occasions: 'Inclusive Democracy and People's Empowerment: The Legacy of Jawaharlal Nehru', speech delivered at International Conference to Commemorate Nehru's 125th birth anniversary at Vigyan Bhavan, New Delhi, 17-18 November 2014 and D.D. Kosambi Memorial Lecture delivered at Ruia College, Mumbai, on 'Jawaharlal Nehru and the Challenges to the Idea of India', 23 February 2015, see also 'Nehru's Legacy', *Economic and Political Weekly*, Vol. 50, No. 16, 18 April 2015.

was a product of the Indian national movement, had to undertake the task of nation-building within the parameters of the basic ideas of this movement, the 'Idea of India' it generated. This is because the post-revolutionary state inevitably bears the imprint of the ideology, strategy, methods, social base and ideals of the movement of which it is a product. In the Indian case it was particularly so because the Indian national movement was a prolonged mass movement (not a coup or a revolutionary overthrow organized by cadre-based 'professional revolutionaries' or 'guerillas' or a 'revolutionary army') which meant that the three basic ideas of the movement, a commitment to a secular and inclusive democracy, sovereignty and anti-imperialism and a pro-poor orientation went deep down into the minds of the Indian people and became hegemonic ideas. The independent Indian state had to undertake the task of nation-building within the parameters of these basic ideas. Nobody could argue that India launch on a path where an authoritarian state would push through rapid development or on a path where India adopt a position of junior partner to one of the superpowers in order to grow rapidly under its umbrella. Anybody who argued such a position would be consigned to the dustbin of history and indeed nobody from the Right to the Left argued such a position at that time.

If maintenance of sovereignty and democracy with civil liberties were two non-negotiables bequeathed to independent India by the Indian national movement, then all efforts at post-colonial transformation in India had to occur within these parameters. However, never before in history was the process of transition to industrialism or the process of primitive accumulation of capital accomplished along with democracy. The Nehruvian attempt at industrial transformation *with democracy* was thus a unique attempt. Nehru was deeply conscious of this and often spoke about it being an uncharted path, 'unique in history'.[9]

The non-negotiable commitment to democracy meant that the necessary 'surplus' required for investment in order to facilitate the transition to industrialism could not be raised forcibly on the backs of the Indian working class and peasantry or on the basis of colonial surplus appropriation as happened in other countries in the past.[10] Nehruvian state intervention and planning was to be *consensual* and not a *command* performance. The path of extracting surplus out of agriculture through land tax or forced collectivization; of forcing surplus out of labour through slavery, indentured labour and in the absence of organized trade union rights or of forcing surplus out of the people of other countries through collection of tribute from colonies, was not open to India. While during colonial rule, the Indian peasant

---

[9]See for example, minutes of the fourth meeting of the National Development Council, New Delhi, 6 May 1955, File No 17 (17&/56-PMS) in *Selected Works of Jawaharlal Nehru*, Second Series, Vol. 28, p.371. See also 'Introduction' in Aditya Mukherjee, ed., *A Centenary History of the Indian National Congress*, Vol. V, 1964-84, Academic Foundation, New Delhi, 2011.

[10]See Aditya Mukherjee, 'Empire: How Colonial India Made Modern Britain', *Economic and Political Weekly*, Vol. 47, No. 50, 11 December 2010 for a detailed discussion of how colonial surplus appropriation aided the process of primitive accumulation in the West.

often ended up handing over more than half of his gross produce as land tax and rent, after Independence the establishment of a democratic regime based on popular will meant that not only was there no tax, or surplus extraction through other forms from agriculture (on which an overwhelming majority of the Indian people were dependent), but a net transfer of income to agriculture occurred through state subsidies. Also, trade union rights to the working class were guaranteed from the very beginning and were exercised vigorously. Of course, the question of appropriating colonial tribute from other countries did not even arise. In fact, even after India won independence, Nehru remained a relentless champion of liberation movements against imperialist domination in other parts of the world.

Similarly, the non-negotiable commitment to sovereignty meant that the transition to modernity could not be accomplished with foreign aid, foreign capital or foreign intervention in any manner that would make India a junior partner of any advanced country, however powerful it may be. The imperative of maintaining sovereignty was a natural pointer towards non-alignment in the post Second World War-Cold War situation where the world was divided into two power blocs. The policy of non-alignment, in other words, was as much a function of the strategy of economic development chosen by India, as it was a product of the Indian national movement's commitment to world peace and sovereignty of nation states.

Industrial Development

Nehru and the early Indian planners had correctly understood that political independence was of little value if it could not be used to acquire first economic and then intellectual independence. At Independence, because of the nature of colonialism she had been subjected to, India was almost completely dependent on the advanced world for capital goods and technology for making any investment. She produced virtually no capital goods. In 1950, India met nearly 90 percent of its needs of machines and even machine tools through imports. This meant that despite political independence, she was completely dependent on the advanced countries for achieving *any* economic growth though investment.

This was a neo-colonial type situation, which needed immediate remedy. And this is what the famous Nehru-Mahalanobis strategy tried to reverse by adopting a path of industrialization based on heavy industry or capital goods industry. During the first three Five Year plans (1951-65), industry in India grew at 7.1 percent per annum. This was a far cry from the de-industrialization of the nineteenth century and the slow industrial growth between 1914 and 1947. More important, 'the three-fold increase in aggregate index of industrial production between 1951 and 1969 was the result of a 70 percent increase in consumer goods industries, a quadrupling of the intermediate goods production and a ten-fold increase in the output of capital goods'.[11] This pattern of industrial

---

[11]A. Vaidyanathan, 'The Indian Economy Since Independence (1947-70)', in Dharma Kumar, ed., *The Cambridge Economic History of India*, Vol. II, Delhi, 1983, p.961.

development led to a structural transformation of the colonial legacy. From a situation where, to make any capital investment in India, virtually the entire equipment (90 percent) had to be imported, the share of imported equipment in the total fixed investment in the form of equipment had come down to 43 percent in 1960 and a mere 9 percent in 1974, whereas the value of the fixed investment in India increased by about two and a half times over this period (1960-74).[12]

This was a major achievement and, as it considerably increased India's autonomy from the advanced countries in determining her own rate of capital accumulation or growth, it created the key condition for non-alignment or relative independence from both the power blocs. In our understanding, no amount of diplomatic finesse could achieve and sustain the objective of non-alignment without the economic basis of relative autonomy having been created. It was this un-structuring of the colonial structure which was to later enable India to participate in the globalization process with considerable advantage to itself.

As India at Independence did not have a sufficiently large indigenous private sector to take on the massive task of developing capital goods industries, the only other option was to develop it through the public sector. The option of basing the development of this

---

[12]These figures are from an extremely persuasive piece by Vijay Kelkar, 'India and the World Economy: A Search for Self Reliance', Paper read at seminar on Jawaharlal Nehru and Planned Development, New Delhi, 1980, reprinted in *Economic and Political Weekly*, Vol. 15, No. 5/7, February 1980.

sector on foreign capital did not arise as the Nehruvian consensus was that sovereignty would be achieved only if industrial development was primarily done indigenously and was not based on foreign capital. The public sector was clearly seen, by a wide spectrum of opinion, which included the capitalists and the Left, as the alternative to foreign capital domination and not necessarily as an alternative to private enterprise, if it was available.[13]

While reducing dependence on foreign capital and technology for making indigenous investment was one way of gaining and keeping the country's sovereignty intact, other strategies were adopted as well. India undertook a deliberate strategy of diversifying its foreign trade so that her dependence on any one country or bloc of countries was reduced. As a result, the geographical concentration index (GCI) of trade with foreign countries declined sharply. GCI of India's exports declined from 0.69 in 1947 to 0.22 in 1975. There was a similar decline in GCI in the case of imports. Significantly, the result of the declining GCI was that the share of the metropolitan countries of the West, which earlier dominated India's trade, declined sharply. For example, the share of UK and USA in India's exports, which was 45 percent in 1947, fell by more than half and by 1977 it was only 20 percent.[14] This was partly achieved by the increase in India's trade with the socialist bloc (which bailed out India at a time when she was extremely

---

[13]See Aditya Mukherjee, *Imperialism, Nationalism and the Making of the Indian Capitalist Class*, Sage, 2002, Chs. 10 and 11.

[14]These figures are from Vijay Kelkar, *op. cit.*

short of foreign exchange by allowing barter and rupee trade) and other underdeveloped countries.

Agriculture

Another area of concern for the maintenance of India's sovereignty and ability to stay non-aligned was India's food security. Indian agriculture had stagnated and even declined under colonial rule and at Independence, India was faced with acute food shortage and famine conditions in many areas. Fourteen million tonnes of food had to be imported between 1946 and 1953. There could be no sovereignty if India was dependent on food aid for its very survival. Indian agriculture needed to be revolutionized and Nehru took up the task on a war footing. It is often wrongly alleged that Nehru ignored agriculture with his focus on industrialization.

Nehru pushed through the extremely difficult task of land reforms in India *within a democratic framework*, basing himself on the long and powerful heritage of the national and peasant movements. A remarkable achievement in contrast to the forced land reforms achieved in Soviet Union or China costing millions of lives or the land reforms of Japan under an army of occupation. By 1957 the back of the over 150-year-old zamindari system was broken. Cooperative and institutional credit considerably weakened the stranglehold of the moneylender. Loans advanced by such institutions increased by more than fifteen times rising from Rs 0.23 billion in 1950-51 to Rs 3.65 billion in 1965-66. Such institutional reforms were combined with major investments in scientific agricultural research, irrigation and electric power projects. A veritable army of Village Level Workers (gram sewaks) and Block Development Officers was spread out in hundreds of thousands of Indian villages trying to provide support and help improve farming methods. Nehru made no false dichotomy between agriculture and industry. Keenly aware that an agrarian transformation was not possible without an industrial transformation, i.e., without electricity, tractors, pumps, chemical fertilizers, etc., he pushed for industrial transformation simultaneously with the agricultural reforms.

The combination of institutional changes (land reforms) and massive state sponsored technological change transformed Indian agriculture rapidly. During the first three Plans (leaving out 1965-66, a drought year), Indian agriculture grew at an annual rate of over 3 percent, a growth rate more than eight times the annual growth rate of 0.37 percent achieved during the half century (1891-1946) of the last phase of colonialism in India.[15]

Attempts are sometimes made to contrast Nehru with his successor Lal Bahadur Shastri, the latter in his all-too-brief tenure being credited with the ushering in of the Green Revolution strategy. The reality is

[15]See George Blyn, *Agricultural Trends in India, 1891-1947: Output, Availability, and Productivity*, Philadelphia, 1966, Table 5.8, p.119; K.N. Raj, *Indian Economic Growth: Performance and Prospects*, New Delhi, 1965 for the pre- and post-Independence figures respectively. See also Mridula Mukherjee, *Colonializing Agriculture: The Myth of Punjab Exceptionalism*, Sage, 2006.

somewhat different. It is clear that by the late 1950s and early 60s, as the benefits from the land reforms that could be carried out in Indian conditions had begun to peak and the possibilities of agricultural growth based on extension of agriculture, i.e., bringing more area into cultivation, were also reaching their limit, Nehru's focus inevitably shifted further towards technological solutions. Even the New Agricultural Strategy, associated with the Green Revolution, of picking out select areas with certain natural advantages for intensive development with a package programme (the IADP or the Intensive Agricultural Districts Programme) was launched in fifteen districts, one for each state, on an experimental basis during the Third Plan in Nehru's lifetime—a practice which was to be generalized on a large scale a few years later. As one of the major scholars of the Green Revolution, G.S. Bhalla, put it:[16]

> The qualitative technological transformation in India—the Green Revolution...came about not during his lifetime but soon after his death. But the *foundations* for the technological development were laid during Nehru's time.

Nehru thus not only brought about major institutional reforms in Indian agriculture, he also laid the foundations for the technological reforms, the basis of the Green

[16]G.S. Bhalla, 'Nehru and Planning—Choices in Agriculture', *Working Paper Series*, School of Social Sciences, Jawaharlal Nehru University, New Delhi, 1990, p.29, emphasis ours.

Revolution, which made India food surplus in a remarkably short period.[17] No wonder, Daniel Thorner, one of the keenest observers of Indian agriculture since Independence, noted:[18]

> It is sometimes said that the [initial] Five Year Plans neglected agriculture. This charge cannot be taken seriously. The facts are that in India's first twenty-one years of independence more has been done to foster change in agriculture and more change has actually taken place than in the preceding two hundred years.

Knowledge Sector

Jawaharlal Nehru was acutely aware of India's backwardness in science and technology, an area deliberately left barren in the colonial period, and therefore made massive efforts to overcome this shortcoming. Focus on scientific education at the highest level was also seen as a necessary part of achieving and maintaining sovereignty by reducing dependence on the advanced world. An unprecedented increase occurred in the educational opportunities in science and technology in the universities and institutes set up in the early years after Independence. Almost all the major

[17]See our chapters (29-33) on Land Reform and Green Revolution in Bipan Chandra, Mridula Mukherjee, Aditya Mukherjee, *India Since Independence*, Penguin, New Delhi, 15th reprint, 2014.

[18]Daniel Thorner, *The Shaping of Modern India*, Allied Publishers, New Delhi, 1980, p.245, addition in brackets ours.

institutions in this area from the IITs (Indian Institutes of Technology), the CSIR (Council of Scientific and Industrial Research), the Bhabha Atomic Research Centre, the National Physical and Chemical Laboratories, the AIIMS (All India Institute for Medical Sciences) and numerous other such institutions were all set up in the Nehruvian era.

National expenditure on scientific research and development kept growing rapidly with each plan. For example, it increased from Rs 10 million in 1949 to Rs 4.5 billion in 1977. Over roughly the same period, the stock of India's scientific and technical manpower increased more than twelve times from 190,000 to 2.32 million. A spectacular growth by any standards, a growth whose benefits India reaps today as the world moves towards a 'knowledge' society, a move which Nehru brilliantly anticipated.[19]

This focus was not counter-poised to primary education as is often alleged. Nehru's commitment to primary education from the days of the 1931 Karachi Resolution drafted by him, which committed the state to providing free and compulsory basic education, remained steadfast. The government system of primary school education during the Nehruvian era is in stark contrast to the near-destruction of that system in today's India where even the poor are increasingly forced to access whatever little education they are able to from

[19]See 'Indian Economy, 1947-65: The Nehruvian Legacy', in Bipan Chandra, Mridula Mukherjee and Aditya Mukherjee, *India Since Independence, op. cit.*

the rapacious private sector. Rather than building on the public education system painstakingly built up in the Nehruvian era, it is either allowed to die, or if not, then active efforts are made to dismantle it.

Nehru's Socialism

Finally, let us turn to the third element of the legacy of the national movement: the pro-poor orientation. Nehru's success in keeping India on the democratic, civil libertarian path against considerable odds (while most other post-colonial countries faltered on this count), by itself ensured that the poor were not altogether left out of the development process or that their condition was not totally ignored. It is now well recognized that democracy is critical for the survival of the poor. It is democracy in India which has ensured that an inflationary path to growth, which hits the poor hardest, was never adopted. The trend rate of inflation in India since Independence had not touched two digits for several decades. No government in India irrespective of their political ideology has been able to ignore the political implications of uncontrolled inflation.

Also, it is democracy and civil liberties that ensured that no large-scale famine deaths could occur in India since Independence—despite some extreme conditions created by climatic shocks—while more than 40 million died in famines in China in the late 1950s and 60s, which the world got to know of decades later because of the absence of a free media. Amartya Sen has emphasized the role of civil liberties and a free press in preventing such mass manmade disasters. With more than 70,000 newspapers and about 700 satellite channels and with nearly thirty newspapers having a daily readership of more than a million, it is not easy to keep famine conditions under cover in India.

While political democracy was understood by Nehru to be a necessary condition for people's empowerment, it was by no means taken to be sufficient. As he put it in 1952:[20]

> If poverty and low standards continue then democracy, for all its fine institutions and ideals, ceases to be a liberating force. It must therefore aim continuously at the eradication of poverty… In other words, *political democracy is not enough.* It must develop into economic democracy also.

Nehru was deeply aware that active efforts had to be made and institutional structures created which would enable the economically weaker sections to achieve a life of dignity. He set up the massive Community Development Programme in 1952 aimed at ameliorating all aspects of people's lives in the remote villages, from improvement in agricultural methods to communications, education and health. His basic objective through this programme was 'to unleash forces from below among our people' by 'creat[ing] conditions in which spontaneous growth from below was possible'. The ultimate aim was 'progressively producing a measure of equality in

[20]*Jawaharlal Nehru: Letters to Chief Ministers* (hereafter *LCM*), 16 June 1952, Vol. 3, p.18.

opportunity and other things'.[21] As a tendency towards bureaucratization began to emerge in this programme, Nehru tried to integrate it with the Panchayati Raj institutions (elected local self-governing bodies) and set up a large programme of cooperatives in banking, marketing and other services benefiting and empowering millions of peasants.[22] Emphasizing the critical role of local village level self-governing, cooperative institutions Nehru said:[23]

> I feel more and more that we must function more from below than from the top. The top is important of course and in the modern world a large measure of centralization is inevitable. Yet *too much centralization means decay at the roots and ultimately a withering of the branches and leaves and flowers.* Therefore we have to encourage these basic organs in the village.

However, the struggle to make these local institutions function in favour of the most deprived was not an easy one in a greatly class, caste and gender divided society. In fact, decades after Nehru passed away, Rajiv Gandhi took the initiative to re-invigorate Panchayati Raj by proposing that elections to these bodies be made mandatory and that the deprived castes, tribes

---

[21]Jawaharlal Nehru, *Speeches*, 5 Volumes, Vol. 2, pp.50-56.

[22]See our chapter on Cooperatives and an Overview of Land Reforms in Bipan Chandra, Mridula Mukherjee, Aditya Mukherjee, *India Since Independence, op. cit.*

[23]*LCM*, 5 July 1952, Vol. 3, pp.38-39, emphasis ours.

and women be given adequate representation in them, which resulted in the 73rd and 74th amendments in the Indian Constitution in 1993. The process of trying to empower the poor and disadvantaged is still carrying on as it must in the future, but the foundation was laid by Jawaharlal Nehru.

Nehru was deeply influenced by Marxism since the late 1920s. His contribution in embedding and then making widely acceptable the socialist ideal of empowering the poor among the Indian people was immense. The fact that not only the communists and socialists but an overwhelming majority of nationalist opinion in India since the late 1930s accepted socialism as an objective was to a great extent because of Nehru.[24] So deeply did this idea get rooted among the Indian people as a whole that as late as 1980 when the decidedly right-wing Jan Sangh, which had nothing to do with socialism or the national movement, was reborn in its new avatar as the Bharatiya Janata Party it chose to declare its creed as 'Gandhian Socialism'!

Nehru was able to give the socialist ideal such wide acceptability in India partly because he made a very early break from a narrow, sectarian and rigid interpretation of Marxism which India's leading historian of the modern and contemporary period, Bipan Chandra, called 'Stalin-Marxism'.[25] Nehru was among the first in the world to

---

[24]See Mridula Mukherjee, *Peasants in India's Non-violent Revolution, Practice and Theory*, Sage, 2004 for a detailed confirmation of this point.

[25]Bipan Chandra, 'Jawaharlal Nehru in Historical Perspective' in *The Writings of Bipan Chandra: The Making of Modern India from Marx to*

make this break from Stalin-Marxism. Roughly at the same time as the famous Italian Marxist Antonio Gramsci, Nehru, in the late 1930s, was groping for a strategy of social transformation in a democratic or semi-democratic framework, which was different from the insurrectionary and violent Bolshevik model that was not suitable for such situations. Nehru was fortunate in being witness to and part of the Gandhian struggle for freedom which was till then and perhaps remains till today 'the only actual historical example of a semi-democratic or democratic-type state structure being replaced or transformed, of the broadly Gramscian theoretical perspective of a war of position being successfully practised'. The fact that Gramsci saw this 'as the only possible strategy' for social transformation 'in the developed countries of the West' underlines the huge significance of the Gandhian movement to the world as a whole.[26]

Learning from the practice of the Gandhian movement made it easier for Nehru to break from the Stalin-Marxist paradigm and argue somewhat precociously that, while there could be no true democracy without socialism, there could be no socialism without democracy. He insisted that civil liberty and democracy had to be basic parts of socialism. The socialist transformation required societal consensus, the

---

Gandhi, Orient Black Swan, New Delhi, 2012 for a brilliant analysis of Nehru, particularly the nature of his vision of 'socialism' and social transformation. Much of what we argue in this section borrows heavily from this and other articles in the book.

[26] *Ibid*.

consent of the overwhelming majority of the people. It could not be a minority revolution led by a band of highly committed revolutionaries, a 'dictatorship of the proletariat'. It was also not enough just to have a majority. To succeed, it had to be socialism acceptable to all sections, by an overwhelming majority. Nehru was anticipating what later events were to validate and what was to be slowly accepted globally by increasing sections of the Left.

By the late 1930s, Nehru began to veer towards the position that socialism could not be brought about by coercion or force. How can you arrive at a consensus by force? He argued that to achieve the desirable end of socialist transformation one should not adopt the means of hatred and violence, and that a socialistic pattern of society could be achieved through non-violent and peaceful means. Fully in tune with the Gandhian notion that wrong means could not achieve right ends, he declared:[27]

> There is always a close and intimate relationship between the end we aim at and the means adopted to attain it. Even if the end is right and the means are wrong, it will vitiate the end or divert us in a wrong direction.

Also, arriving at a socialist consensus would mean that one would have to view it as a process and not an event arrived at in a 'revolutionary moment'. This

[27]Jawaharlal Nehru, *Speeches*, Vol. 2, p.392 quoted in *Writings of Bipan Chandra, op. cit.*

would have to be a long-drawn-out process with its ups and downs, a process which may have to at times slow down, moderate or tone down its immediate goals, in order to carry the bulk of the people along, including those who held opposing positions. Nehru, writing from prison as early as the 1940s, described his understanding of how the National Planning Committee (NPC), set up by the Congress in 1938, should move in a socialist direction:[28]

> ...it became clear to me that our plan (NPC)... was inevitably leading us towards establishing some of the fundamentals of the socialist structure. It was *limiting* the acquisitive factor in society... It was based on planning for the benefit of the common man, raising his standards greatly, giving him opportunities of growth...And all this was to be attempted in the context of *democratic freedom* and with a large measure of *cooperation of some at least of the groups who were normally opposed to the socialist doctrine.* That cooperation seemed to me worthwhile *even if it involved toning down* or weakening of the plan in some respects.

Evident here is the notion of taking steps in the socialist direction (rather than establishing of socialism by the immediate overthrow of the existing structure) and of doing so within the democratic framework, accepting the logic of adopting such a framework by taking steps,

---

[28]Jawaharlal Nehru, *The Discovery of India*, Asia, 1961, p.400, emphasis ours.

including partial compromises, which made it possible to carry along a wide section of society.

Nehru was to retain throughout his life this nuanced persuasive style of functioning while remaining resolute in his goals, which brought him the support, love and admiration of the millions in a manner which was surpassed only by Gandhiji. And as a true disciple of the master, while appealing to all sections of society, he succeeded in keeping his gaze focused on the poor, the oppressed and the disadvantaged. His great achievement was that he got a very large part of Indian society, individuals and institutions to share his socialist vision. In the Nehruvian period, from the planning commission and the public sector bureaucracy to the media and popular films, the socialist objective was seen as a desirable one, not defined in any narrow fundamentalist way but as Nehru broadly outlined it.

The economy that Nehru inherited did not generate enough resources to launch major anti-poverty measures, yet poverty declined impressively. In the early years after Independence the biggest anti-poverty measures were the steps taken towards land reforms, creating credit and other services cooperatives, investment in public health and education and later the Green and the White revolution (cooperative movements in milk production and distribution).

Today, half a century after his death, with infinitely higher economic capacity to empower the poor, when we falter hopelessly on this count, we realize how important it is to remember Nehru's legacy. With more than twenty-five years of high growth rates hovering between

6 to 9 percent, with enough resources to launch some of the world's biggest anti-poverty programmes like MGNREGA (Mahatma Gandhi National Rural Employment Guarantee Act), India still has a totally unacceptable situation of more than 300 million people in poverty, 46 percent of our children malnourished and one out of three children of school-going age out of school! The Human Development Index for many parts of the country is below that of Sub-Saharan Africa. On top of all this, attempts are now being made by the current regime to starve of funds the MGNREGA and other programmes such as the ICDS (Integrated Child Development Services) aimed at reaching minimal nutrition, education and health to the poorest.[29] The obscene level of inequality and crony capitalism prevalent today was inconceivable in Nehruvian times.

Evidently while Nehru's legacy in keeping India's sovereignty intact has survived and the secular-democratic structure despite very serious recent challenges to it still holds out, the chief failure has been in the equity front. The Indian elite by and large has turned its gaze away from the poor, once again forefronting the need to return to Gandhi and Nehru and create popular movements to keep the 'Idea of India' alive in its fullest sense.

[29]See, for example, Neerja Chowdhry, *Indian Express*, 30 March 2015; Mani Shankar Aiyar, 'Jaitley's Budget is for Sahib Log' and 'BJP Pushing Economy Towards Disaster', in NDTV.com, 2 March and 10 March 2015.

disagreed with Nehru's conviction that how Pakistan treated its Hindu minority population could in no way determine India's attitude towards its own minorities, especially Indian Muslims. He had also aligned himself with outfits that championed Hindu communal and revivalist issues.

In a bitterly fought election, Purushottam Das Tandon won the presidency of the Congress. To Nehru, having as president someone who held and articulated views which were at variance with the ideals of the party was not at all a welcome proposition.[17] Writing to B.C. Roy he declared that he was readying to fight it out: it would either be Tandon's line or his that would hold in the Congress.[18] For him the party was his own home as well as the chief instrument with which to make the larger home, i.e., a democratic, secular and inclusive independent India. Through the party, and as prime minister, therefore, he was trying to give certain broad directions, certain approaches to fulfil long cherished goals: that, like the party, India would be for the underdog, and that it would be non-communal.[19] The aim was not only to remove barriers to development but also to create a society of equal citizens.[20] To allow any deviation from these core

[17]Jawaharlal Nehru to P.D. Tandon, 30 March 1951, S. Gopal, (ed.) *Selected Works of Jawaharlal Nehru*.

[18]Jawaharlal Nehru to B.C. Roy, 17 August 1951, *ibid*.

[19]*Ibid*., Vol. 16, p.162.

[20]Presidential Address, *ibid*., p.210.

Trustingly, JN

Gopalkrishna Gandhi

His trusting nature, it has been said, was a weakness in Prime Minister Jawaharlal Nehru.

A prime minister, in a democratic order, is elected. He holds office at the pleasure of the people. But he is, nonetheless, a political behemoth. No one equals him; none may dream of exceeding his power or glory. He is, in that, no different from kings of old. Sun-dried wisdoms say he should expect let-downs, betrayals, deceit. He should be prepared for the shock of treachery, the sting of calumny. And so whether or not he is a lion in majesty or an elephant in magnificence, he must ever be a jackal in canny opportunism, a hyena in cold-blooded ruthlessness. Rather than 'noble', he should be 'sharp'.

Nobility, the politically seasoned would say, is for saints not prime ministers. Saints might repose trust in people, not a prime minister. He should not rely on others, certainly not be seen relying on them. Others should rest on the prime minister, not the other way round. Faith, hope, reliance are what he must evoke, not extend to others. Trust is far too naïve an emotion for a prime minister to yield to. And, for the matter of that, a prime minister should have no emotions. That is what a political pragmatist would want a prime minister to be.

And that is what Jawaharlal Nehru was not.

Trust as First Principle

Nehru trusted, quite unreservedly, people and institutions to play their roles honestly. As prime minister he trusted officials, colleagues, to fulfil their mandates diligently. As his own external affairs minister he not only trusted India's diplomats to be experts of their method but also exemplify the ideals of the newly decolonized world. As minister in charge of the portfolio of science and technology he expected—trusted—scientists to be men and women of science in the fullest sense of that term, not just people holding university degrees in science.

He trusted legislators in the country, whether from his own party or those from the Opposition, to be democrats first and 'Party' MPs (Members of Parliament) or MLAs (Members of the Legislative Assembly) only thereafter. He wanted them to be democratic not just in name but in deportment, bearing and intent. He trusted Parliament itself to be both a historically-minded maker of new laws and a sensitive tribune of the people.

Judges he trusted to be just, fair. But more, he trusted them to interpret and apply the law in ways that he, as a freedom-fighter who had stood in British docks, had expected them to be—in the dock themselves, the dock of Time. Son of a lawyer and a lawyer himself, he expected lawyers to be serious, not flippant and certainly not fraudulent.

Journalists, he knew, should be unfettered, but can they be, can they afford to be, irresponsible? No! He thought they should be, can be and will be what the great denizens of London's Fleet Street were—frank, fearless but wholly accountable to facts. Cartoons and cartooning he loved. 'Don't spare me, Shankar!' he could tell the most merciless of all Indian sketching satirists. The reason was he trusted Shankar's nibs to dip in ink, not bile.

Above all, he trusted the people of India to try to adjust their step and time their gait with what he thought was the progress of humankind into modern ways. He trusted them to move away from preoccupations with what he regarded as stagnant, backward. Straining the farthest limits of credulity he trusted fellow Indians, uninitiated as they were in empirical rigour, to share his enthusiasm for what he termed 'a scientific temper'.

Trust as Second Nature

Prime Minister Nehru carried a map in his mind. And a planetarium as well.

He had an inborn awareness, surprising in one born to a self-centred household in a land-locked town, of the coasts and coast-lines, mountains and tree-lines of the world. He had a sense of the stars, both as a navigator might and an astronomer.

He saw the world planetally and, so, undividedly.

The earth for him had a curious destiny as a little sphere that went about on its axis with its own laws of rotation and progress. Its denizens were earthlings before they were anything else, so distributed over its surface as to have evolved in their own distinct ways, grouped together within naturally-formed tracts, getting into conflicts and battles where the strong prevailed but the weak did not get forgotten, rising above their misfortune and adversity. Politics was for him a method of self-assertion and self-protection in an environment where competition and conflict had grown into an art and a habit.

Politics for him was a method for people to organize themselves for better living conditions, greater scope for physical and intellectual advancement. And nationalist politics were a variant of the same. Had Nehru not been waylaid by national politics in India he would have made a professor of the natural sciences, a tutor who kindled wonder and nudged venture. But politics, nationalist politics, abducted a future don.

As prime minister of India this earth-gazer opened his map and his sky-screen with the eyes of a trusting student. He started by reposing trust in the country's neighbours. 'Don't!' warned his Deputy Prime Minister Sardar Patel, 'That way lies danger.' Those were not the Gujarati pragmatist's precise words but that was the purport of the famous letter he wrote to the prime minister on China's monumental presence on India's north-eastern borders. In advice that sounded like it came from Kautilya or Tiruvalluvar, he urged the prime minister to have the borders patrolled and watched by the Intelligence Department.

Nehru trusted his instincts about Asian solidarity, Afro-Asian unity. Likewise about India's democratic affinity with the 'free world' on the one hand, and its socialist affinity with nations led by the USSR (Union of Soviet Socialist Republics), on the other. He trusted the Commonwealth and despite opposition from many, remained consistent about the advisability of India's being part of it. The democratic nature of the organization and its freedom from racial bias was sufficient reason for him to keep the link and value it. He trusted the United Nations to be and do all that he thought it was meant to be and do.

Instinct made him non-aligned between the two superpowers before non-alignment became his foreign policy's cornerstone. And it was the same instinct that made him, non-alignment's mentor that he was, to yet shun the role of a hierarch among non-aligned leaders.

Distrust

If Nehru trusted instinctively, he permitted himself in no uncertain terms certain forms of distrust.

In politics, he was uncomfortable with anything over which hung the odour of fascism or of communalism. In the world of the intellect, he was impatient with the doctrinaire and the prescriptive. In the world of the spirit, sanctimonious claims to divinity and supernatural powers jarred on his nerves.

But even in these 'no trust' areas, his reaction was that of irritation and impatience, not intolerance. The democrat in him obliged him to share political space with even those and that which he distrusted.

I will attempt, in the following pages, to see the place of trust and trusting as well as of instinct and its cousin, intuition, in the arena of Nehru's prime ministership.

Trusting Persons

There are those who start on the basis that a person can be trusted until shown to be otherwise, and those who start with scepticism. Nehru clearly belonged to the first kind of people.

A photograph taken in the late 1940s by the Calcutta-based photo-artist Jayant Patel has Nehru and Sardar Patel looking at a piece of writing. Standing in a close knot, Nehru is the very picture of trusting optimism, Patel of cautious pragmatism. Nehru seems like he has accepted what he is reading, Patel is giving it a close look. While Nehru trusts, Patel seeks evidence. While Nehru seems to be ready to believe, Patel seems to want proof.

Khara ya khota?—real or fake? The question would, for Nehru, most likely end with, 'He seemed quite trustworthy, certainly not a charlatan…Well, we all learn, don't we…?'

By and large (a phrase, incidentally, that Nehru would use quite often, with its equivalents like 'more or less', 'in large measure', 'substantially') Prime Minister Nehru's trust in people was not betrayed. In other words, he did not regret the confidence he reposed in people.

In a word-counting essay only representative descriptions are possible. So I will choose here, from among the many persons Prime Minister Nehru trusted, by instinct, to do right, three who just happen to be Malayali: V.K. Krishna Menon, an old friend and 'his' first high commissioner in London, K.R. Narayanan (K.R.N.), who rose to be President of India, and M.O. Mathai, his private secretary.

Menon and Narayanan were slightly acquainted with each other in London. When Narayanan finished his course of study in London with a First Division, the then small Kerala community there threw a party in his honour and High Commissioner Krishna Menon was invited to be the chief guest. Leaning on his walking stick at the doorway Menon said to him, 'So, Narayanan, I hear you have got a First. You know, some people get it by a fluke.' If Narayanan was staggered it was only for a moment. He responded with, 'Is that how you got yours?'

K.R.N.'s term at the London School of Economics (LSE) is deservedly celebrated for the equation he enjoyed with the cerebral but morally intense Harold Laski.

I was privileged to serve President Narayanan as his secretary and once, while returning from Parliament House to Rashtrapati Bhavan with him after his ceremonial opening of the Budget Session in 1999, he related to me the following: 'When I finished with LSE, Laski, of his own, gave me a letter of introduction for Panditji'. So on reaching Delhi I sought an appointment with the PM. I suppose, because I was an Indian student returning home from London, I was given a time-slot. It was here in Parliament House that he met me. We talked for a few minutes about London and things like that and I could soon see that it was time for me to leave. So I said good-bye and as I left the room I handed over the letter from Laski, and stepped out into the great circular corridor outside. When I was halfway round, I heard the sound of someone clapping from the direction I had just come. I turned to see Panditji beckoning me to come back. He had opened the letter as I left his room and read it. "Why didn't you give this to me earlier?" "Well, sir, I am sorry. I thought it would be enough if I just handed it over while leaving." After a few more questions, he asked me to see him again and very soon I found myself entering the Indian Foreign Service.'

This was trust, this was confidence, not just in a person but in India's ability to find the right persons for the right responsibilities. Narayanan's diplomatic career, taking him through the diplomatic missions of India in Bangkok, Ankara, Beijing and Washington was to bring him to his natural bent for political work, to Parliament, to the Council of Ministers, India's vice presidency and then its presidency.

Nehru's trust in Krishna Menon belongs to a different category altogether. Political analysts have tried to decode it with the axe of frontal assault and the nail-file of curious probes. It is clear that Nehru's confidence in Menon was instinctive and intellectual, a matter of feeling and of reason. The personality concordances between the two do not interest me so much as the political fluxions. The nature of Nehru's political trust in Menon came from his finding a thought-partner in Menon, one who shared with him the same template of ideas, with understanding and commitment. The template is locked, to be drawn from but not modified, enriched by interpretation, never interfered with in the carving.

Nehru found in Menon someone he could rely upon to represent his aspirations for independent India both in the United Kingdom and then in the UNO (United Nations Organization). Menon could and would accentuate the Nehru line in his own syntax, his own polemics but in the same vocabulary. More, he found in Menon one who could crucify himself in the cause. 'What he accomplished on the international scene, as India's spokesman and envoy, and indeed as the voice of the nations emerging from colonial rule into independence,' writes Enuga S. Reddy, 'is not fully understood and recognized even in India.' Explaining how Menon was called 'Mouthpiece Extraordinary and Troublemaker Plenipotentiary' (*Life*, 25 October 1954) Reddy tells us how Menon 'never bothered to defend himself against such attacks and even seemed to relish the attention he received'.

Nehru could not have trusted better or more rewardingly.

To quote Enuga Reddy again, 'He hit back with passion when India was slighted.' This, for Nehru, was important, even crucial, for India was at that time being treated by many opinion-makers and policy framers in the United States as a third-rate power whose destiny could be no more than that of a satellite of the United States.

No two men could be more different and think

more alike than Nehru and Menon. They shared a sense of history that wanted to see India count. They resented, with passion, any slights to India, be it by 'small' neighbours or by 'big' powers. The fact is Nehru could be no less angry if not angrier than Krishna Menon, but was careful in the way he expressed it. Krishna Menon was sharp in his language.

Far more difficult to appreciate is Nehru's trust in M.O. Mathai, his private secretary who joined him as India was becoming free and worked with him, almost like a shadow, for nearly fifteen years. Before I say something by way of an attempted analysis of this trust, I may be allowed an anecdote. Like most urban children, I went through a phase when stamp-collecting was my hobby, my passion. My father used to get a modest number of letters every day and the envelopes used to become my property, along with the stamps on them, coming in rich and colourful variety from different nations. When my father died suddenly—I was about twelve then—my stamp collection came to an abrupt halt. I took recourse to the very pitiable and philatelically low-grade method of buying stamps from vendors, to augment my drastically reduced collection. One day someone said to me, perhaps mischievously: 'Why don't you ask Panditji to send you a small number of stamps each month? He was such a good friend of your father.' I was a little abashed by the thought: Panditji? Oh no…how can I ask him…he should not be troubled…But then a kid is a kid and a passion is a passion. And this particular kid, a future bureaucrat, was sufficiently clerical of mentality even then. I figured that my writing to the PM with such a request being out of the question, I should try a less absurd proposition and must go to the proper channel. So, getting the contact details for his private secretary who, I gathered, was a certain Mr M.O. Mathai, I sent to that, to me, unknown functionary my hand-written rather plaintive request. The very next day, I got a fat bundle of stamps drawn from the envelopes of the prime minister's daily dak, hand-delivered at home. I was, to say the least, overwhelmed. My mother believed that M.O. Mathai must have checked with Panditji and that it was Panditji himself who had ordered the bundle to be sent to the stamp-collecting son of his late friend. But I was sufficiently babu-minded even then to realize that Mr Mathai would have acted on his own, that Panditji handled what was inside the envelopes that came to him, his staff could do what it liked with the envelopes.

I was struck by three things: First, by the sheer bounty of the generous favour. Second, by the kind-heartedness of the private secretary. Third and most importantly, by the thought: What an extraordinarily powerful man this PS must be in that he has either persuaded the PM to oblige this random kid or has the autonomy to act thus, on his own. Two other thoughts also occurred to me. Children think more complex thoughts than we imagine. First: Mr Mathai is obviously as privy to all the PM's dak, as we were in our family, to my father's. Second, that perhaps the PM's grandsons are not into philately, else Mr Mathai would have sent this bundle of stamps to them, not to me. Be all that as it may, I was so overwhelmed that I wrote back a letter of thanks to Mr Mathai in which, at my mother's suggestion, I also said the stock of stamps was such as to make up for a whole year's collection and that he need not take the trouble of sending me any more. But, if I remember aright, he did send two or three more bundles.

I never ever saw Mr Mathai and very soon forgot all about stamp-collecting. But looking back, I find that episode very revealing. Here was a man who meant something to his boss. He must have had something in him, at the very least, a sharp brain, to make him so valuable to the PM, so essential to his office. I therefore hold it to be a pity beyond words that circumstances led to M.O. Mathai's turning into a sour individual whose reminiscences, perhaps teased out of him by Nehru-baiters, ended up as little more than potsherds of his broken ego.

M.O. Mathai is the Malvolio in Nehru's *Twelfth Night*, distrusted, disliked, and ultimately, self-demolished. He could have become an editor and commentator, giving invaluable analyses, supported by sources both published and unpublished, of the Nehru years, which could have become the equivalent of the Transfer of Power papers.[1]

There are others Prime Minister Nehru trusted, with no regrets to mar the reposing. President Rajendra Prasad he respected with reservations, President Radhakrishnan he trusted without any. And with good cause! If Prasad

---

[1]A 12-volume set of documents on the transfer of power from the British rulers to India, and the partition of India.

during all his twelve years as president had just one prime minister—Nehru, Radhakrishnan in his single term saw three—Nehru, Lal Bahadur Shastri and Indira Gandhi, smoothing the transition with his courageous, calm and sagacious oversight. How Indira Gandhi reciprocated that by working in the shades and half-lights of political manoeuvre to deny Radhakrishnan a second term as president, is recorded in Sarvepalli Gopal's biography of his father.

If trust was Nehru's guiding principle and operational method, distrust was his daughter's first and last emotion. Her supporters might cite the fatal exception of her trusting the security picket in her residence to establish the superiority of suspicion over credulousness.

Nehru trusted his daughter's instincts and her intelligence. We may never fully know in how many or which matters he, as prime minister, was influenced by Indira Gandhi's advice. We do know that she gave him the democratically gross advice to dismiss the first communist government of Kerala in 1959. His going against his own principles and precepts and his trusting her wisdom in that matter constitutes a stain on his prime ministership. The Congress' winning the election held in Kerala after the CPI (Communist Party of India) government's dismissal consolidates the canniness of her advice, not its integrity.

Nehru's trust in persons was mostly well placed but when ill-placed, it brought dire consequences. For he trusted wholly and did not withdraw it peremptorily. He was too much of a gentleman to do that.

Trusting At Home

Crossing what he called 'the moat of Indian poverty' was Prime Minister Nehru's priority. The Gandhi era of the freedom struggle could have led to no other prioritization. The sequencing of founding precepts in the Preamble to the Constitution of India reflected that orientation. 'Justice, social, economic and political', precedes Liberty, Equality and Fraternity in that conceptual atrium. The Ambedkar stewardship of the Constitution's drafting too could have done with nothing less. Nehru trusted all limbs of the state to pass through that portal feeling proud and awed, joyous and responsible. To a large extent his trust has been vindicated. He would be proud of the number of poverty-addressing enactments that have passed through legislative crafting, judicial review, and are now part of the Indian state's law-book. He would be proud too of the honing of the electoral process in India which has made it the world's most vibrant democracy.

His trust in universal adult suffrage, with no qualifications of the educational or property type has been more than vindicated, with every community in India sending representatives to elected bodies. But apart from the brand there is such a thing as the quality of the product. Nehru would have been scandalized by the infusion of money, white, black and grey, into India's election process. Equally by the intimidation of the voter. Every weakness in the Indian condition, be it of gender, caste or illiteracy is shamelessly exploited, every fault-line widened, at election time. And compounding that is the shameless addition of a naked communal content in electoral messages. Prime Minister Nehru would never have imagined that rule by majority would, by a perversion of its logic, nourish the most bigoted argument of Hindu Rashtra. This is where his trust has met its greatest betrayal, so to say, at its own hands.

A legitimate political majority becoming the argument for a completely illegitimate religious majoritarianism would have seemed impossible in a Gandhi-Nehru-Ambedkar derived political system. But not so any more. With a portrait of Veer Savarkar beaming its blessing from the Central Hall of Parliament, a BJP-majority government need not distance itself from programmes that are avowedly Hindutva in orientation. To put it in Einstein's cadence, Nehru would have scarce believed that such an ideology in flesh and blood would ever walk upon this democracy.

Was the Constituent Assembly, then, a gathering of the innocent making a Constitution for the good?

Trusting Abroad

Sardar K.M. Panikkar, the historian and Nehru's ambassador to China, is no favourite of Indian nationalists. It is believed that he lulled Nehru into complacency about China's intentions. Before examining that assertion, it would be good to reflect on an important observation made by Panikkar in his 1959 appraisal of Nehru. He was no longer India's ambassador to China and the Sino-Indian War had not yet happened, when Panikkar wrote: 'Anyone who studies his work as the prime minister of India can easily see that not only in his internal politics but in the formulation of his external policy he is dominated by a sense of history… the Chinese revolution to him is a major aspect of the resurgence of Asia—a historical formation of outstanding importance in this century.'

I believe as ambassador, K.M. Panikkar did not go wrong in his assessment of our national interest. His prescriptions, as ambassador, for the handling and safeguarding of India's border interests vis-à-vis China are unfairly judged against the events of a decade later. They should be tested against the Sino-Soviet, Sino-Indian, Indo-Soviet and Indo-US dynamics of the time he made those prescriptions in. The dividends in terms of international credibility and our effectiveness in the United Nations, during the decade 1950 to 1960 owes not a little to the fact that there was, despite known differences over the border, substantial goodwill between the two great Asian powers. Bandung, Brioni and the great efflorescence of the non-aligned movement during that first 'clear' decade of the Cold War, would have been impossible if India and China had been pitted against each other, and the Soviet Union forced to take one or the other side, to the glee of John Foster Dulles.

Nehru trusted world history.

What kind of a trust is that?

It is, well, just that. Nehru believed that humankind was evolving, be it in Russia and China through their revolutions or on the African continent through its great transformation. Likewise, he had great visions of and for Latin America. He trusted history to be moving, not in a very organized fashion, or with a coordinated goal, but nevertheless moving, towards a just world order.

The freedom of India and the decolonization process he viewed from that larger perspective of the inevitability of better conditions.

In his enthusiasm for that beckoning goal, he did not see that great and horrible distortions could take place within those revolutions, as happened in Stalinist USSR or under the Cultural Revolution and the 'Gang of Four' in China. Won over by the example of Vietnam's Ho Chi Minh, he could not have foreseen a Cambodian Pol Pot. He knew of the dangers of 'new power' and famously ticked off Ghana's Kwame Nkrumah with 'What the hell are you doing putting your head on a stamp?' But by and large he had a rather roseate view of world history's grand march, just as he had great and touching confidence in the wholeness of India's political evolution.

The year 1962 was to change that for him rather suddenly and cruelly.

Trusting Nehru

And that is when India's trust in Nehru also began to alter.

On the 1960s 'reappraising Nehru' bandwagon, clambered on right-wingers, left-wingers, intellectual idlers, political busybodies, do-it-quick biographers, do-it-slow researchers, all claiming to have seen through the first prime minister's supposed 'dreaminess', his 'out-of-touchness'.

Today, more than half a century after 1962, Nehru-baiting has found renewed energy in the shape of a political machoism that suggests that it is effete to trust and smart to look sharp. That puffed-chest thumping view looks at politics at home and diplomacy abroad as an exercise in plain cleverness. Trust, in that way of thinking, begets disappointment, weakness and worse.

Gandhi and Nehru are sought to be typecast, plaster-cast, as symbols of an age of innocence that has been overtaken by the age of the real, the actual. For a while more, I believe, this propaganda—for it is nothing else—will work. But sooner than the propagandists believe or expect, their bluff will be called for the so-called 'real' is a pneumatic myth perpetrated by political hierarchs and social patriarchs for reasons of power-grabbing. It will be punctured by its own defeat at the hands of the Preamble to the Constitution which it is so cynically ignoring.

Historians—true historians, not manipulators of history—can go wrong. They are not perverse. Nehru was wrong, quite wrong, often enough for us to say in his own style, 'What the hell are you doing putting your stamp on unworthy heads?' But he was in Gandhi's words, 'pure as crystal'.

Trust may be too trusting. Of that a prime minister should be careful. But better by far to trust and be shocked into correction than to mistrust and lead a nation through the gospel of suspicion.

Remembering Nehru in the Dark Times

Shabnam Hashmi

The partition of the country had a deep impact on my family. My father, Haneef Hashmi, was a student leader and had spent many years in jail for fighting against the British. His family decided to move to Pakistan when the country was divided. He refused to go. My grandfather's flourishing furniture business at Kashmiri Gate collapsed not long after. The violence that followed Partition disrupted all economic activity. The demand for furniture in embassies and universities, to which my grandfather too was a major supplier, dried up, gradually reducing the family's circumstances. It came to a point where my mother had to sell leftover wood, nails and iron from the decaying factory just to feed the children. Though our family, like many others, lived in abject poverty, the spirit of the freedom movement never died. The British Raj had left India ransacked in its wake, and we were part of the impoverished nation which now had to be rebuilt.

In 1955, while still dealing with major financial crises, my father was invited to Aligarh to work in the university by the then Vice Chancellor Zakir Husain, who knew him well. The family finally left the Delhi house, once the epicentre of political debates and cultural *mehfils*, and moved to Aligarh. The house was later occupied by others—and no attempt was ever made to recover it. I was born in Aligarh in 1957.

We didn't have enough to spend lavishly on food or even to wear decent clothes, but the stories we heard, the poetry that reached our ears, the literature that our parents made available at home, which was often beyond their means, kept all of us connected to the ground. We heard stories of the Indian Independence struggle, we heard about Nehru and Gandhi, we heard stories about the Second World War, fascist Germany, and we talked about the Idea of India and the dream of building an equal society. Our physical needs never overwhelmed us as we shared a dream that was more powerful. It was a dream of humanity, peace and kindness.

My first physical encounter with Jawaharlal Nehru was in 1963, when he came to Aligarh for the Sir Syed Day celebrations. There was a huge cricket ground there which was prepared for the helicopter's landing. All of us went there to get a glimpse of our first prime minister. A huge crowd was waiting for him to arrive. As the helicopter started descending, people began cheering but then had to step back amid the din and the dust that it stirred up. Jawaharlal Nehru greeted the people gathered as he came out of the helicopter, shaking hands with them. My father, an extremely handsome man, stood out among the crowd in his white sherwani and white pyjamas. Nehru saw him and shook hands with him. That day my father refused to wash his hands or shake anyone else's!

But my mother was not happy in Aligarh. My eldest sister Sabiha was growing up, and people's comments about her wearing frocks and what she ought to be wearing instead irked my mother. She decided to move back to Delhi. In 1964, she took up a job in Delhi as the principal of a nursery school and soon all the children joined her, though the entire family was reunited only in 1969 when my father too got a job in Delhi. We lived in tiny rooms and shared houses for quite a few years till my mother was allotted government accommodation.

One such room that we—the five siblings and our mother—shared was in Nauroji Nagar. With us used to live my mother's colleague Lalita didi, her sisters and a brother. The landlord and his family lived in the other room. I was six years old and tagged along with my mother to her nursery school. My other brothers and sisters went to different schools. My mother's school was close to Nauroji Nagar so we would return earlier than my siblings. My father was still working in Aligarh and apart from his weekly visits there was virtually no other way to communicate with him. If for some reason he was unable to come on a weekend, a postcard would arrive.

We were at home when we heard some altercation between Sabiha and Sohail. Sohail had come rushing back from the neighbour's house and told Sabiha that he heard on the radio that Jawaharlal Nehru had died. Sabiha gave him a tight slap and asked him not to speak nonsense. But she went to the neighbour's house nonetheless as they had a transistor, and heard the news for herself. Indeed songs being aired had been stopped in the middle and an announcement made about Nehru's death. She came back wailing. I had never seen Sabiha cry. My mother was in shock and began crying too. Soon Sohail, Shehla, Safdar and other people from the neighbourhood joined them in mourning. I found myself crying too though I did not understand the gravity of the situation. This was 1964. There were no televisions in Indian homes. The neighbour's radio-set was our only source of information. The rest of the day was spent listening to various news bulletins on BBC, which was considered the most authentic radio channel in those days. The usually vibrant atmosphere in the neighbourhood transformed into a deeply melancholic one, as if life had come to a grinding halt. The hustle and bustle in the markets stopped, people spoke in soft, low voices, and the loudspeakers were silent. Even the vegetable and fruit sellers, who were used to shouting loudly, didn't announce their arrival in the neighbourhood.

Early in the morning the following day all of us left for India Gate with Bhai Sahib (our landlord). There were about fifteen of us including our family, the landlord's family and Lalita didi with her siblings. Finding our way through the crowd was a major task. I vividly remember those moments, both sides of the Rajpath were swarming with people. We moved onto

King George Avenue, now called Rajaji Marg. I was the tiniest and could not see anything. Bhai Sahib lifted me onto his shoulders to give me a better view of the mammoth crowd and the last journey of the beloved leader. As the car cavalcade reached the place where we were standing and passed us by, people started crying, some stood with folded hands, some saluted the departed leader and many shouted slogans like '*Chacha Nehru Amar Rahein*'. Jawaharlal Nehru's body was kept on an open army truck. His head was kept higher than his feet so people could see his face. I managed to see his face too, and his hands folded at his chest. There wasn't single man or woman around us whose eyes weren't wet. It was estimated later that close to two million people bade farewell to Nehru on Delhi's roads that day.

I was too young to understand the loss. It was much later, when I entered high school and we had a chapter in our English textbook called 'The Light Has Gone Out of Our Lives', Nehru's speech on Mahatma Gandhi's assassination, that I started relating to Nehru.

'The light has gone out of our lives,' he said, 'and there is darkness everywhere. I do not know what to tell you and how to say it. Our beloved leader, Bapu as we called him, the Father of the Nation, is no more. Perhaps I am wrong to say that. Nevertheless, we will never see him again as we have seen him for many years. We will not run to him for advice and seek solace from him, and that is a terrible blow, not to me only, but to millions and millions in this country. And it is a little difficult to soften the blow by any other advice that I or anyone else can give you.'

As I read these lines, written about Mahatma Gandhi, I recalled that day. I travelled back to that melancholic atmosphere and realized that another light had gone out of millions of people's lives on 27 May 1964, and there was darkness everywhere.

*

I was neither an avid reader nor intellectually inclined and ended up not engaging in higher academic activity. I got involved during my college days in teaching girls and women who had never been to school. So before I could ever start exploring the possibility of reading Nehru, Gandhi or other stalwarts of our freedom movement, I was fully engaged in working among the underprivileged with little time to spare. While I lost the opportunity to learn from the writings of these great men and women, I was exposed to the stark discrimination that existed in our society.

I find myself not competent enough to write about Nehru or Gandhi with any authority. I make this attempt on the basis of whatever little political understanding I have developed in the course of my work as an activist among the ordinary people of our country.

When I remember my childhood and even the later years till I finished school and compare them with today, what strikes me most is the loss of serenity. I miss the calmness and peace. I miss the aesthetics. This cacophony hasn't increased overnight. It has grown consistently over the past few decades. It is also not the case that the grotesque behaviour on display in our public space has replaced dignified discourse overnight.

I must have revisited Nehru's 'Tryst with Destiny' speech hundreds of times in my life: 'At the stroke of the midnight hour, when the world sleeps, India will awake to life and freedom. A moment comes, which comes but rarely in history, when we step out from the old to the new, when an age ends, and when the soul of a nation, long suppressed, finds utterance. It is fitting that at this solemn moment, we take the pledge of dedication to the service of India and her people and to the still larger cause of humanity.'

When I compare India awakening to life and freedom, stepping out from the old to the new, dedicating itself to the cause of humanity, to the present day, where freedoms are supressed and the past is glorified, where in the name of humanity we release convicts of gang rape and murder and felicitate them, I shudder to think about the future of my beloved country. As a six-year-old I did not for a second feel afraid surrounded by thousands of ordinary men and women who had come out to pay homage to Nehru. When I compare that sea of humanity to the crowds who surround innocent cattle farmers and lynch them or to the crowds who came, packed in trucks, and attacked, raped and looted in 2002 in Gujarat, I am forced to say that this is not the India where I was born and grew up.

When I compare Jawaharlal Nehru's vision—who brought in the 1954 Special Marriage Act, realizing that young people from all religions, communities and castes would soon begin reaching the institutions of higher education, which were being set up across India in the initial years after Independence, and meet each other and fall in love, and would need the protection of the law against the still conservative society which will not let them choose their own life partners—to the present-day Romeo Squads set up to hound young couples, I feel extremely sad for the younger generation. Their right to choose what they want to eat and wear, what they want to speak and whom they want as their life partners are all under severe attack.

I quote again from Nehru's speech: 'The service of India means the service of the millions who suffer. It means the ending of poverty and ignorance and poverty and disease and inequality of opportunity. The ambition of the greatest men of our generation has been to wipe every tear from every eye. That may be beyond us, but as long as there are tears and suffering, so long our work will not be over.'

These were not *jumlas*, mere rhetoric. Jawaharlal Nehru gave concrete form to his vision. He spearheaded India's economic growth. The Planning Commission was set up in 1950. The first Five Year Plan aimed at improving the economic condition, making better use of the country's resources, and improving agriculture to produce more, to provide employment and to save resources for future investments. It aimed at a growth of 2.1 percent GDP but ended up reaching a growth rate of 3.6 percent. Along with improvement in the agricultural sector, there was lesser inflation but also better employment opportunities. By the end of the first Five Year Plan, five new IITs (Indian Institutes of Technology) were opened. The second Five Year Plan focused on industrialization and heavy industry. Steel plants were set up in Bhilai, Durgapur and Rourkela. The Atomic Energy Commission and the Tata Institute of Fundamental Research were set up. The Plan aimed at a 25 percent rise in national income and was able to achieve 20 percent. It had targeted a growth rate of 4.5 percent and was able to get to 4.27 percent. Nehru, through this growth model, was targeting the 'millions who suffer' and trying to end poverty.

When I compare what was happening in the Nehruvian era for the upliftment of the poor and making India self-reliant to today's situation where, according to the Oxfam *Inequality Kills* report, India is described as a very unequal country where the 'richest 98 Indians own the same wealth as the bottom 552 million people', it becomes very clear that India has drifted far away from Nehru's declaration that '[t]he ambition of the greatest men of our generation has been to wipe every tear from every eye'. It is also very clear that India is no longer governed by the greatest men of our generation!

India's long independence struggle against the British produced thousands of great men and women. They fought not only for the freedom of the country but also for building a society which would be equal, just and humane. A society where everyone will be treated with dignity irrespective of caste, class, gender, the language they speak or the region they belong to. They celebrated diversity, they celebrated love and they celebrated progress.

Nehru said in that same speech, 'The future beckons

to us. Whither do we go and what shall be our endeavour? To bring freedom and opportunity to the common man, to the peasants and workers of India; to fight and end poverty and ignorance and disease; to build up a prosperous, democratic and progressive nation, and to create social, economic and political institutions which will ensure justice and fullness of life to every man and woman. We have hard work ahead. There is no resting for any one of us till we redeem our pledge in full, till we make all the people of India what destiny intended them to be. We are citizens of a great country on the verge of bold advance, and we have to live up to that high standard. All of us, to whatever religion we may belong, are equally the children of India with equal rights, privileges and obligations. We cannot encourage communalism or narrow-mindedness, for no nation can be great whose people are narrow in thought or in action.'

Today, we are faced with a situation where we are governed by those whose political and cultural forbears were not even part of the struggle; they were not part of this dream, and not only did they support the British but watered the seeds of hatred sown by colonial rule. Hatred and bigotry cannot produce great men or women. Hatred can only produce bigoted individuals. During the last few decades we have witnessed their factories of hate brainwashing the populace, snatching away the capacity of the young to think, to analyse, to reach their full intellectual potential, retarding their capacity to examine an argument on its merits, churning out, as a result, mediocre, insensitive, uncaring and even violent individuals. The capturing of hearts and minds and letting only one kind of information enter them are very dangerous signs for a society.

Jawaharlal Nehru wrote in *Discovery of India*: 'So long as India kept her mind open and gave of her riches to others, and received from them what she lacked, she remained fresh and strong and vital. But the more she withdrew into her shell, intent on preserving herself, uncontaminated by external influences, the more she lost that inspiration and her life became increasingly a dull round of meaningless activities all centred in the dead past.'

Not content with the brainwashing of the youth, we have the Rashtriya Swayamsevak Sangh (RSS) outfit Arogya Bharti running its 'Garbha Vigyan Sanskar' project to produce tailor-made babies—*uttam santati*. Started from Gujarat, it is now expanding to other states as well. The RSS ideologue M.S. Golwalkar had praised Hitler in 1938 thus: '...to keep up the purity of the Race and its culture, Germany shocked the world by purging the country of the Semitic Races—the Jews. Race pride at its highest has been manifested here'. The RSS agenda, likewise, includes both the purging of 'impure races' and producing fair, tall, Sanskrit-speaking babies—a disturbing echo of Hitler's dream of blue-eyed and tall babies.

I wonder if these tailor-made babies will ever relate to our *Chacha* Nehru, whose birthday we celebrated as Children's Day and millions of children continue to every year.

During my childhood, the imprint of Nehru's vision

could be seen in every sphere of life. Nehru did not think only about industrialization and encouraging science and technology. He strongly believed in and propagated a scientific temper. To quote again from his *Discovery of India*, 'The scientific approach and temper are, or should be, a way of life, a process of thinking, a method of acting and associating with our fellowmen. That is a large order and undoubtedly very few of us, if any at all, can function in this way with even partial success. But this criticism applies in equal or even greater measure to all the injunctions which philosophy and religion have laid upon us. The scientific temper points out the way along which man should travel. It is the temper of a free man.'

It thus becomes necessary, for those who govern India now, to invisibilize and demonize Nehru. If they need to control critical thinking, spread obscurantism and provide a scaffolding to hoary superstitions, demolish all democratic structures, suppress the press and human rights defenders, then Nehru, his vision and his writings present a difficult obstacle.

It is important to understand that the Sangh is doing its work and doing it very systematically. They have never been this close to converting a secular, democratic and diverse India into an authoritarian Hindu state. They will leave no stone unturned to fulfil their dream.

It is for the ordinary citizens of India to decide how they will defend Nehru and Gandhi's legacy.

My Quotidian Companion

(The Common Man's Nehru)

Kiran Nagarkar

I am deeply conscious of the fact that I am not a Nehru scholar, a student of politics or economics nor an authority on post-Independence India. Undoubtedly I am singularly unqualified to speak of our first prime minister. As they say, beware of your friends, they are the ones who will get you into trouble. When one of them whom I respect enormously insisted I write an essay on Nehru, I agreed very reluctantly since a 'no' was not an option. For a while I thought I would do a short stint of intensive research and try to pass off as an old hand at Nehruviana. But of course I would be exposed immediately since this book was bound to have many fine Nehru scholars writing about him. It occurred to me then that since the time that I have memories of the past, Nehru has been by my side. I couldn't possibly have anything new to add to Nehruvian scholarship. At best what I can offer is a highly personal interaction with the man since I have spent hours and days talking to him, debating policy matters with him, disagreeing with him, but more often than not humbled by his pragmatic idealism albeit in a rather one-way conversation.

Here's my rough Nehru timeline.

My First Encounter with the Prime Minister of India

I must have been ten or twelve at the most when I was sent to the hill station called Lonavala during the summer holidays with one of my father's friends who was the principal of a school called Gurukul. Looking back it would appear I had forgotten to take any reading material with me. Or perhaps I was hoping to find something worthwhile in the school's library. If that was the case I was mistaken. There was no library. As a school student today would say, no problem, yaar. There was a copy of Jawaharlal Nehru's door-stopper, *The Discovery of India*, on a shelf in my room. Yes, that was going to be my vacation reading. I trust you are by now convinced that I was a child prodigy. I am not quite sure who I was trying to impress. My hosts? They were mostly not there. I doubt that they were even aware of my superior reading tastes. Maybe my target-audience was the great author himself though I suspect the only one who was in awe of me was me. Reading that book was like plodding through concrete that was about to set. I am sure I didn't get beyond page forty but hey, I was running into words like monotheism, iconography, polytheism, the Upanishads, maybe even teleological or ontology. Does it matter that I had no idea what these polysyllabic words meant? Frankly, I am amazed I didn't go off both reading and the writer of the book permanently.

Encounter Two

Years passed, I was doing First Year Arts at St Xavier's in Bombay (as Mumbai was known then). I had already made my mark in the world and got into the Guinness Book of Records. I failed in every single subject except moral science in my terminals. (It continues to be a mystery to me why morals are considered a matter of science. And I am still not sure about the answer to the first question this science asks, 'Who made man?')

I improved upon my earlier performance enormously during the finals. I didn't appear for a single paper. I got smallpox despite having been vaccinated in childhood. Once again I was without a book to read unless I was to bone up on the execrable civics or geography textbooks.

There I was lying in bed with high fever and the knowledge that if I survived I would be marked for life with pockmarks and anyone I ran into would turn his head away at my sieve of a face. Oddly enough the only book I could lay my hands on was Louis Fischer's *Mahatma Gandhi, His Life and Times.*[1] To this day I find it difficult to understand what a book on Gandhi was doing in our house. Oh, make no mistake, we were 100 percent Congress followers but Mahatma Gandhi was not one of my father's favourites.

[1]Pub. Jonathan Cape, London, 1951.

I have no idea if books can change lives, a bit far-fetched if you ask me. But Fischer's life of Gandhi was a revelation and it remains so even today though hundreds of biographies and studies have appeared since then. I cannot to this day forget the impromptu speech Nehru delivered on the radio the night Gandhiji was murdered. It was without flourish and without any rhetoric. It came straight from the heart and sixty-seven years later, it still feels like someone had slipped a knife into your own heart.

> 'The light has gone out of our lives and there is darkness everywhere and I do not quite know what to tell you and how to say it. Our beloved leader, Bapu as we call him, the father of our nation, is no more. Perhaps, I'm wrong to say that. Nevertheless, we will not see him again as we have seen him these many years. We will not run to him for advice and seek solace from him, and that is a terrible blow not to me only but to millions and millions in this country. And it is difficult to soften the blow by any advice that I or anyone else can give you.
>
> 'The light has gone out, I said, and yet I was wrong. For, the light that shone in this country was no ordinary light. The light that has illumined this country for these many years will illuminate this country for many more years, and a thousand years later that light will still be seen in this country, and the world will see it and it will give solace to innumerable hearts. For,

that light represented the living truth, and the eternal man was with us with his eternal truth reminding us of the right path, drawing us from error, taking this ancient country to freedom.'

Fischer's book was my discovery of Gandhi, Nehru and India. The two leaders moved in with me then even though I was in quarantine and have stayed with me all these years.

Encounter Three

Nineteen fifty-six was the year for crucial internal changes in India. After winning independence, we had remained a jumble of former principalities and the rest of the subcontinent. We were a huge, unwieldy country and difficult to manage and an intelligent division of it into several states was overdue. Nehru appointed the States Reorganization Commission to tackle the tricky question of the basis on which these boundaries should be drawn. The Commission chose the various languages of the country to define the formation of states and soon Parliament had approved the new formula. Initially the intention was to leave the former Governor's province of Bombay which included both Gujarat and Maharashtra, intact, with a few additions.

The people of Maharashtra and I suspect of Gujarat too, however, wanted their own separate states. There were protests and agitations in Bombay and elsewhere which sometimes turned violent. Four or five people in Maharashtra lost their lives, I am not quite sure if these were accidental deaths or these folks actually participated in the protests, but they were later declared martyrs. I remember that the Union finance minister at the time, C.D. Deshmukh, resigned because of this issue and finally in 1960 Maharashtra and Gujarat were given independent statehood. I remember not seeing eye to eye with the PM for a long time on this score. There were bound to be, I felt, other less divisive solutions. Some folks felt that the country could have been divided into north, south, east, west and central provinces to avoid linguistic bitterness. It would take years for me to understand that even by dividing the subcontinent into twenty-five or thirty units, some states were just too big to manage. Besides, any other solution, too, would raise the hackles of one section or another in the country. As I see it now, Nehru was wise to opt for the linguistic formula since it was perhaps the least problematic though both local political parties and even litterateurs have used their mother-tongues to ostracize other tongues and persecute their speakers.

Encounter Four

Most of the time I was immune to news in my youthful days but 1956 was also the year of the tragic Soviet invasion of Hungary. The local population's revolt was heroic but the results were a foregone conclusion. The Soviet tanks and troops rolled into the cobbled streets of Budapest and other cities and towns and crushed all signs of resistance. Nehru's response was muted. Politics had trumped a moral stance. At age fourteen, I was not unaware of a fledgling democracy's weaknesses and dependence on Soviet leadership, not to mention the need to be circumspect but that didn't prevent me from suffering a case of ethical discomfiture.

It was much later that I learnt that Nehru's emissary in the United Nations (UN), Krishna Menon, acting independently and before receiving instructions, abstained from voting on a resolution condemning the Soviet Union for the use of force.

Encounter Five

Come 1962, it was India's turn to be invaded. The culprit was one of our closest friends of the time, China. I was at the Dadar Tram Terminus Circle in Mumbai some years earlier when Chou en-Lai's cavalcade had passed through. For some reason I have distinct memories of the Chinese premier standing upright in the open official car, a pale-skinned figure dressed in the grey uniform worn by all Chinese officials including Mao in those days. The much-touted slogan of the times was *Hindi-Chini bhai bhai*. That was the brief golden age of Nehru's philosophy of Panchsheel[2] which had garnered us the friendship of the leaders of the non-aligned nations: Nasser of Egypt, U Nu of Burma, Tito in the former Yugoslavia, Sukarno of Indonesia and Mao's China. The *bhai-bhai* would soon sour into bye-bye.

The Chinese invasion was seen in India almost unanimously as the great Chinese betrayal. Our soldiers

---

[2]See p.47, footnote 19.

were totally inadequately prepared for the below zero temperatures. They had no warm clothes and whatever weapons they had, were obsolete. They froze in the Himalayan heights and they were thrashed. Along with the rest of India I too developed an acute distrust of China which continues till today. Recently some foreign journalists have maintained that Nehru was solely responsible for the tragedy. Where does the truth lie? Somewhere halfway in between? After all there were several bones of contention. We had given asylum to the Dalai Lama and his people and that didn't sit well with the Chinese who had already occupied Tibet. The other major problem was Arunachal Pradesh which the aggressors believed fell in their territory while we in India are convinced it is ours. Whichever way you look at it, there are going to be conflicting partisan views and the chances of a consensus are unlikely.

Nehru never recovered from the Chinese debacle. I remember him coming to the Brabourne Stadium in Mumbai. The poet Pradeep had penned a song which C. Ramchandra had composed and Latabai had sung on that occasion: *Jo shaheed hue hai unki, Zara yaad karon qurbani* (Those who have suffered martyrdom, give a thought to their sacrifices). It was bruited that Nehru had tears in his eyes. Perhaps he could not forgive himself for the loss of over two thousand Indian jawaans in that twenty-day war.

Encounter Six

Nehru died on 27 May 1964. Life in Mumbai came to a standstill. That night my friend Kumar got his

Dodge convertible out and five of us friends headed for Lonavala. There was hardly any traffic on the road. It was after midnight when we got a room in a cheap hotel. We were hungry but had to wait till next morning to get something to eat.

Didn't I feel guilty, you may well ask, taking off when my PM had passed away? No, no guilt at all. What was I going to do at home? Fast? Pray? Meditate on the futility of life? No, I didn't need to make a show. Besides, I was still discovering him and anyway grief is a strange business, you never know when it hits you. When my mother died a couple of years earlier, I'd get fed up of visitors who would come to condole and for whom I'd then have to make tea. I told my brother I was going to see a flick and went to Metro cinema to watch Gregory Peck in *To Kill A Mockingbird* along with two friends. A few days later there was a quiet prayer meeting and in the middle of it someone said, 'They called her Mai,' and I had to bend low to hide the tears which wouldn't stop flowing.

Life After Death

Isn't it perverse and not merely curious how often we understand the value of some people and their crucial importance to our daily lives as well as our worldview only when we are deprived of them? Since Nehru's death we are together often, very often. Oddly enough with the passage of years I have grown much closer to him. And along with him I realize acutely the debt our country owes to him, Sardar Patel, Maulana Azad,

B.R. Ambedkar and that whole generation of leaders and thinkers.

1964: The change of guard after Jawaharlal Nehru's death was surprisingly smooth. Lal Bahadur Shastri took over the reins of the country. Offhand he was not an impressive man but Shastri was no easy walk-over. He was mild-mannered but there was steel in him. The year 1965 was when Pakistan and India fought their second war. The reason as almost always was Kashmir. The war lasted seventeen days and peace was brokered by the UN. Unfortunately Shastri died in Tashkent after having signed the Tashkent Pact with Field Marshall Ayub Khan.

As always there was a pointless debate about who won the war. The truth is, both lost. It would be interesting, to say the least, to speculate what form our democracy would have taken if Lal Bahadur Shastri had lived longer, much longer, but it would also be an exercise in 'What if' futility.

1966: Once again the Congress and the people of India had to perforce embark on a search for a new prime minister. One of the strongest contenders was Morarji Desai, a man from the old guard, honest, humourless, holier-than-thou, a martinet and ambitious. Perhaps the Cabinet members and the Congress Working Committee (CWC) felt safer with a less threatening or domineering candidate. They chose Jawaharlal Nehru's daughter, Indira Gandhi, who had been information minister during the Shastri regime. Sometimes old adages make good sense, at least in retrospect: better a known devil (like Morarji) than an unknown one. Suffice it to say that she betrayed her father and his democratic ideals time and time again. She was unscrupulous, devious, utterly focused on the pursuit of power, ruthless, and unforgiving.

Encounter Seven

Two years after I joined an advertising agency in 1968, I was asked to do two campaigns for Hindustan Machine Tools, or HMT for short. One was a corporate campaign for the company and their full range of tractors, printing machinery, metal forming presses, die-casting and plastic processing machinery, and the other, a product campaign for their range of heavy-duty presses. It was the first of my many encounters with Jawaharlal Nehru's vision of India in my adult years. Let me underline the fact that what I gained was not an overnight insight. Quite the contrary. It was a slow accretion over decades and a process of understanding the far-sightedness and wisdom of the late PM's all-encompassing game-plan for the country.

We were a fledgling nation and there was an acute shortage of money but Nehru had got his priorities right. The nation had to be built. And what it needed was a solid industrial base. And that's exactly what Nehru set about building with his trademark single-mindedness. HMT was established in 1953, not even six years after we gained independence. It was in many ways the cornerstone of the substantially large investments the country made in industrial foundations. Bharat Heavy

Electricals Limited and Bharat Earth Movers Limited were both incorporated in 1964. Many other state-funded and managed industries like steel plants were established around that time.

Come the 1990s, it became fashionable to think of Jawaharlal Nehru as the villain for going the socialist way and getting the state involved in industry instead of leaving it to private enterprise as the capitalist systems do. His detractors held the view that but for him, this country would have made far more progress. (Here, an aside: do we understand that socialism and communism are very different beasts? For a substantial period Britain practised socialism and the country had free medical services, free education and unions to fight for the fundamental rights of the working class.) If socialism is the bête noire of the current generation, then obviously we are meant to understand that capitalism is the panacea and a far better system. So then it follows that the better system led to the collapse of the world economy in 1929 and 2008 and rewarded US bankers like Johnny Dimon of JP Morgan Chase who were the main culprits with a 74 percent raise and a much higher bonus? And not a single one of them was sent to jail under the bizarre justification that institutions like the banks were too large to be allowed to fail. There's some major chicanery at work here. The financial institutions failed because of these unscrupulous bosses at the top who indulged in all kinds of dubious practices. Removing them would surely introduce the concept of accountability and make the operation of these institutions much more transparent and safer. Incidentally it is the considered opinion of many highly-regarded economists that mixed economies with strict regulatory oversight do far better.

Perhaps a reminder of the history of pre-Independence times and 'the Bombay Plan' might have given these wise people, who come down so heavily on Nehru and socialism, pause and a sense of perspective. Proposed by a group of Indian industrialists, J.R.D. Tata and J.D. Birla amongst them, in the early 1940s, the plan suggested that given the limited resources at the disposal of private industry and the need for India to become competitive in the international arena, government participation was absolutely essential in infrastructure development. Let me quote Manmohan Singh, the former finance minister who opened up the market in the early 1990s and later became the prime minister: 'As a student of economics in the 1950s and later as a practitioner in government, I was greatly impressed by the "Bombay Plan" of 1944. In many ways, it encapsulated what all subsequent plans have tried to achieve…Above all, it defined the framework for India's transition from agrarian feudalism to industrial capitalism, but capitalism that is humane and invests in welfare and skills of working people.'

There's no gainsaying the fact that many of these state-run companies in later years were perpetually in the red and a heavy burden on the exchequer since they were mismanaged, their equipment and technology utterly outdated and never streamlined. And they suffered from those two deadly diseases: zero accountability and corruption. They certainly needed to be either drastically reformed or closed down but to lay the blame at Nehru's door requires a deeply prejudiced mindset and a crass mendacity. The man died in 1964 and we would like to blame him for what's happening in 2014.

1975: Indira Gandhi was at the height of her popularity after the Indo-Pak war of 1971 when we defeated Pakistani forces and an independent Bangladesh came into being. She won the next elections but was unseated from the PM's post because of a judgment that revolved around a technical point. Overnight, she proclaimed an Emergency unbeknownst to even her own Cabinet and appropriated all power in her own hands. Most of the Opposition leaders and some members of her own party were imprisoned but she didn't stop at that. There was total censorship and all fundamental rights guaranteed by the Constitution were abrogated. Her sense of insecurity even amongst her own party members and chief ministers was so acute, she removed many of them. The only person she trusted was her younger son, Sanjay, and that was the start of the Gandhi dynastic rule.

Her father had persuaded us to think that the only way political life could and should be conducted was on the basis of the Constitution of the country which guaranteed democratic rule and the fundamental rights of each and every citizen regardless of caste, affluence or gender. Emergency rule declared these principles null and void. It may be a cliché but even today we don't seem to have learnt that the price of democratic freedom is perpetual vigilance.

Encounter Eight

The year is 1976 or 1977. The advertising agency Arun Kolatkar and I were working for had gone bust two years earlier and since no one was willing to employ us, we were freelancing. Out of the blue the Tata Institute of Fundamental Sciences called us to do an audio-visual show for their visitors, some of them Nobel Laureates. Dr Ramani of the computer science department had been assigned to brief us. 'Every country,' he told us, 'needs a place to think.' That was distilled Nehru. The man thought long and deep and even in prison wrote thoughtful books and letters laying out his vision and elucidating it.

Nehru was an excellent judge of character and had the gift of delegating power to men who were as far-sighted and driven as he was and were able to deliver. Plus he knew precisely how to get the most out of people for the benefit of the nation. Some time before Independence, Nehru had spotted Homi Bhabha when they both happened to be in Paris. Over the years he had kept an eye on the young atomic physicist as a man of potential. Bhabha assisted Nehru in the planning of the atomic energy plant in Mumbai but his main interest was to establish the TIFR (Tata Institute of Fundamental Research) with the help of Nehru and J.R.D. Tata. TIFR was allotted one of the best sites in Mumbai at the southern edge of the city right next to the sea. Under Homi Bhabha it attracted the finest talent from all over the world and put India on the world map of science.

It was Nehru who endeavoured to put education in our country on a sound footing which would help us compete with the best in the world. Early in his premiership it was decided to start Indian Institutes of Technology (IITs) in eighteen cities. The IITs were meant to draw the best talent as well as represent the highest standards of education in the country and were regarded as national centres of learning. Nehru's idea of knowledge, history and the sciences was a trifle different from that of the current PM, Narendra Modi, who spoke recently of our glorious past when our ancients apparently already knew how to transplant an elephant's head on to that of a child whose head had been lopped off.

Encounter Nine

I had been to Chandigarh while I was still at school. The architectural prodigy that I must have considered myself was not overly impressed with the new city. The next time I was in Chandigarh was fifty years, may be more, later. My reaction was very different this time. The partition of the country had seen the influx of hundreds of thousands of refugees into the subcontinent. (We often forget it was no different on the other side.) It was the new government's responsibility to find them a home and housing. Many of the displaced settled down in different parts of India. Jawaharlal Nehru's sheer audacity paid rich dividends. He came up with a unique answer to the problem. He asked the legendary Le Corbusier, the Swiss-French architect, designer and urban planner, to design and build a brand new city from scratch. The rationale was a truly insightful one. The refugees were a terribly traumatized group of people. A whole lot had lost some or all their family members. Many others had lost their limbs. And all but all of them had lost their homes, their property, their jobs, their livelihoods and witnessed horrible scenes of carnage, rapes and crimes.

Chandigarh, as Nehru envisioned it, would be a new beginning, utterly unconnected with the past and would thus help to alleviate if not erase awful memories. Corbusier's Chandigarh would be India's very first contemporary city and its geometric grids would perhaps serve as a paradigm for older cities hoping to modernize and expand. Today Chandigarh and its clone Bhubaneshwar are thriving new metropolises which have re-worked some of Corbusier's concepts, not always for the better but it remains a daredevil act for India. The traffic flows smoothly, there's room to grow, there are playgrounds, there's plenty of housing and there's a lovely artificial lake and the air does not asphyxiate you. The one amenity oddly missing is a public transportation system, especially a metro. Hopefully one of these days the local government will wake up and ensure a fine metro system.

Nehru's Role in My Writing

I cannot pinpoint precisely how my novels, plays and non-fiction reflect Nehruvian thinking but I have little doubt that my writing is shot through with the values I inherited from him, not to mention Gandhiji, Patel, Ambedkar and other leaders of the Freedom Movement. My play *Bedtime Story* is not only an indictment of the Emergency that Indira Gandhi had declared but its centre of gravity is located firmly in the democratic values that her father stood for. Nehru abhorred the notion of entitlement. It was during the Emergency rule that I articulated my personal credo of responsibility: 'Anything that happens anywhere in the world, whether it is in our backyard, Iraq or Venezuela, you and I are responsible for it.' Both those cop-outs called 'What-can-I-do' and 'apathy' are anathema. We have to stand up and raise our voices; for not to do so is to be party to the crime.

The central premise behind everything that Nehru stood and fought for was the sanctity of human beings. The CWD (Central Works Department) chawls in my novel *Ravan and Eddie* were a leftover relic from British rule. On the face of it, *Ravan and Eddie* is about two communities, Catholics and Hindus. There's no hostility between the two but neither is there any rapport or amity. The adults won't cross over and break the ice. It is left to the two young boys to change the paradigm. But the novel was also an oblique plea for human dignity. Obviously the only objective of the colonizer is to exploit the colonized. But once we gained independence, I believed that in time our government would ensure that the poor who stayed in the chawls would get a fair chance at living with dignity. Every poor family would not only have a roof over its head but its own toilet and bathroom; plus water on tap and air and light. So much for my pipe dreams. The Brits had gone home but our own leaders demonstrated that they too could colonize and exploit the downtrodden and the deprived.

It is a tragic irony that the greatest betrayal of our first prime minister came from his own family, the Gandhi dynasty. Indira Gandhi was murdered by one of her Sikh security guards. Her son Rajiv Gandhi took over as the next prime minister and his very first act was to ignore the massacre of thousands of Sikhs in Delhi alone as it was taking place in real time. And then to justify the mass murders at a rally some days later, by quoting a pathetic adage: 'When a big tree falls, the earth shakes', instead of bringing out the military to scotch the terrible systematic massacres with an iron hand. It's something of a mystery how the new PM came to be known as Mr Clean after these vengeful murders of a whole community for the crime of one man. After the demolition of the Babri Masjid, Mumbai saw the ghastly 1992-93 massacres. This time the victims had a familiar name, Muslims. Come 2002, Gujarat witnessed horrific murders, once again of Muslims.

Where had Jawaharlal and his legacy of secularism disappeared? Did the leaders who were present when these atrocities took place not remember that we won independence with a non-violent, civil disobedience movement invented by Gandhiji and emulated by hundreds of thousands of our countrymen, as well as Martin Luther King Jr, and Nelson Mandela? How was it that now we were happy to murder our own? Most importantly where was the idealism which had sustained us in a prolonged struggle for swaraj? Nehru died in 1964 and yet we keep killing him and his remarkable ideals. I tried to address these concerns in a novel called *God's Little Soldier.* My protagonist Zia is a brilliant man but as his brother tells him, 'You are good man gone terribly wrong.' Zia is an idealist who forgets that however noble the end, the wrong means cannot justify it.

Let me recall a few very brief sentences in a re-imagining of the life of Kabir within *God's Little Soldier.* This is what Kabir says: 'There is only one god. And her name is life. She is the only one worthy of worship. All else is irrelevant.'

I cannot pay Jawaharlal Nehru a greater compliment.

[*NB:* Even as I started writing my first novel in Marathi I had realized that there were two subjects I would never be able to touch: one was Shivaji and the other, Subhas Chandra Bose. Both were highly complex and intriguing figures and hugely tempting to grapple with but beyond taboo as far as I was concerned. Shivaji because of the Shiv Sena shibboleth and Bose because the nimbus of hagiography around him was so dense, no one dared to talk about the time when he seems to have lost his ethical compass and began cultivating the most heinous and murderous fascist leaders of the time.

Bose now is suddenly big in the news. The current BJP regime has released selected excerpts from surveillance allegedly conducted by the Nehru government against Bose's family. The media have gone to town quoting Bose's kin and making all kinds of scurrilous insinuations against Nehru. The government has, as is its wont, trotted out its favourite bogey, the national interest (read the RSS agenda) for not publishing the full documents. Dictatorships obfuscate and survive on innuendoes and cloak-and-dagger intrigue. Democracies, on the other hand, do better with that oxygen called the unvarnished truth.

By now the Indian public is familiar with the fact that Gandhi is invoked today only in the context of the Swachh Bharat campaign and that too only in terms of sweeping the trash and litter but never about Gandhi cleaning toilets routinely for that is a no-no and something best not mentioned since the implication is that it's Dalit territory. But there's complete amnesia when it comes to Gandhiji inventing and spearheading the unique concept of a non-violent, civil disobedience freedom movement. As to Nehru he is persona non grata today. But it's evident now that the tactics have changed and the new strategy is to malign and smear his name.

There is something deeply troubling about the way our countrymen have for decades refused to face certain truths about Subhas Chandra Bose. No one can deny that while he was with the Congress he was a wonderful and charismatic leader but things went totally haywire as he began to have military and dictatorial ambitions from 1928. While Gandhiji, Nehru, Patel and the other leaders of the Freedom Movement abhorred Mussolini and Hitler and all that these two fascist leaders stood for and the havoc they had wrought (bear in mind that one is not even referring to the holocaust because its true horrors and dimensions would be revealed only at the end of the war), Bose was an ardent admirer of these two monsters who embodied all that was evil in mankind. There was an element of the juvenile in his belief that my enemy's enemy is my friend. If that was not bad enough, he was all set to join hands with the advancing Japanese armies. Again, he misread the nature and the consequences of a Japanese occupation. Few countries were as unconscionably brutal and cruel as the Japanese. And what they wanted was territorial expansion. Did Bose really think the Japanese would do us a favour and hand over the country to us? All we would have gained is a switch from one colonizer to another. In a speech given in 1943 in Singapore and printed in a newspaper, he said, 'For a few years at least [he had mentioned the figure twenty in a previous sentence], after the end of British rule in India, there must be a dictatorship.' Perhaps that's the reason why the political bosses at the centre today feel such kinship with him.

It might be a good idea if one paused for a minute and asked oneself just one question: what if Hitler or the Japanese had won? The British would indeed have begun to look like saints and saviours compared to the Nazi Germans and the ruthless Japanese of the Second World War.]

The Final Tally

This is the 125th anniversary of Jawaharlal Nehru's birth. Some weeks ago there was a fifty-minute panel discussion on Nehru on NDTV. There were four speakers, one of whom was a learned, bespectacled middle-aged gentleman who hogged most of the TV-time on that particular night. He had a lot, no, that's the wrong word, he had only negative things to say about our first PM. Fair enough, I thought, there are few things more damaging to a genuine appreciation of a person's work and contribution than hagiography and hero-worship. Perhaps I might get a better perspective on Nehru's role and contribution to the country from a solidly argued critique. I think I will just reproduce his brief peroration for you to get a feel for his scholarship, honesty and worldview. He had obviously practised that last bit. You could see how pleased he was with himself as he delivered his final glib but deadly blow. 'Nehru was an aesthete and a stylist. That's all that he was.'

What is it that makes our extreme right-wing intellectuals incapable of speaking with the integrity, analytical clarity and sense of balance that even your worst enemy deserves? But let them stew in their own pettiness of mind. Did aesthetes and stylists win independence for our country? Even India's enemies will grant that we won independence in a manner unknown till that time. Indian leaders like Gandhiji, Nehru, Patel, Rajendra Prasad and their thousands of followers had to be out of their minds to believe that they could take on the mightiest empire in the world with a new and risible weapon called non-violent civil disobedience. But they did it and we are the incredibly fortunate recipients of the fruits of their idealism, courage and perseverance. Gandhiji, Patel, Nehru, Ambedkar, Maulana Azad and most of the other leaders were exceptionally heroic men. During the massacres of Partition, they would walk fearlessly into crowds wielding swords, knives and thirsting for blood, and with the force of their personalities and plain dedication establish peace and sanity amongst the masses.

The word 'plebiscite' used in the context of Kashmir at the UN is considered Nehru's biggest error, the one that has continued to haunt his legacy. But show me a man who doesn't make mistakes and you need no longer look for God. Let's not forget there's no advanced training institute for prime ministers. Nehru was a greenhorn when it came to governing a country, a subcontinent really, that was faced with innumerable crises after its birth. Bush, Obama, Churchill, de Gaulle and every prime minister or president in the world has made blunders at one time or another. Those who followed Nehru as prime minister have only made the situation infinitely worse by turning Kashmir into a police state in all but name and by a brutal military and highly intrusive occupation. I believe, perhaps naïvely, that the Kashmir issue can still be resolved to the benefit of all three parties. Give the Kashmiris autonomy and let both Pakistan and India stop interfering in their internal affairs. Instead let both the countries on either side invest in the well-being of the Kashmiris and turn that earthly paradise into the bridge of peace between India and Pakistan. Obviously this is going to be incredibly difficult given the rabid fanatics on either side. But it can be done if the two countries have enormous resources of patience and persistence in the face of seemingly irresolvable differences and daunting problems and ill-wishers. And they would have to negotiate secretly as successive prime ministers of the UK did with the parties in Ireland for long years.

Even if you ignore Nehru's extraordinarily rich vision for our country, the actual creation of a diversified industrial base and how quickly he put the subcontinent on a secure footing, his greatest contribution will always be embodied in the fact that he made us all believe in democracy despite endemic illiteracy, poverty, caste and class barriers and ensured that we practised it as if it was in our genes.

One look across the border at our desperately beleaguered neighbour, Pakistan, not just in the early years but even today, should be enough to achieve a sense of perspective and the debt we owe to Nehru's democratic vision. Think about it. Jinnah died soon after he became the prime minister of Pakistan. Since then for the greater part of the sixty-eight years since Independence they have had military rule. Ayub Khan, Zia-ul-Haq, Pervez Musharraf have had no qualms declaring *coups d'état* repeatedly and dismissing democratically-elected governments. The army is delighted with the billions which America pours into their coffers despite the fact that the CIA and various other American agencies have pointed out that most of the aid goes either into the pockets of the military top brass or is utilized for financing anti-American or anti-Indian-and-Afghanistani activities.

As for a strong industrial base, most of their equipment used to be imported. It's no different today. I recall being in Karachi in the early 1980s for four days. India had only three makes of cars, Ambassador, Fiat Padmini and Standard Herald in those days. Pakistan had many brands of cars, all of them imported. I am sorry but my heart doesn't bleed for all those Indians whose short-sightedness and desire to own fancy foreign cars would have come at the cost of a crippling dependence on a foreign power. Even in the few areas where Pakistan is self-sufficient now, the majority of industries are owned by the military. Apart from that, we know that about a handful of families own most of the wealth in Pakistan. If that is not bad enough, the enmity between the Sunnis and the Shias is a major killer along with the daily terrorist attacks.

In Egypt the military owns over 70 percent of the industries. If Hosni Mubarak was a stupendously corrupt military despot, Abdel Sisi is far worse. The Egyptian judiciary, which is obviously a creature of the military, condemns a hundred and fifty to two hundred people in one go in trials where the accused have no say. Journalists who are one of the pillars of a democracy are thrown into jail. If all this does not give us pause, look at what is happening in many African countries. Beware what you wish. Hopefully we don't want to become the new Africa, Pakistan or Egypt.

Nehru must have done something right, very right. The armed forces in India are entirely under the control of the civilian government. The BJP could come to power with a nearly absolute mandate in June 2014 because of Nehru's idea of India and democratic rule. The man who spoke about Nehru being 'an aesthete and stylist' could do that because Nehru's idea of a democracy did not believe in gagging people.

So long as we allow democracy to breathe freely, I think this country should do okay.

Panditji: Icon, Symbol, Emblem

Syeda Hameed

My very first 'recollection' of Pandit Jawaharlal Nehru goes back to a time before I was even born.

It was in Srinagar where my father, Khwaja Ghulam Saiyidain, was Director, Education, of the princely state of Jammu and Kashmir, from 1938 to 1945. One day there was much excitement in the house because Father had invited Panditji for tea. In his autobiography, *Mujhe Kehna Hai Kuch Apni Zubaan Mein* ('I Have Something to Say, in My Own Way'—the first line of a couplet written by his grandfather, the poet Altaf Husain Hali), Father writes that the state government, on instructions from the Centre, asked him not to go ahead. He refused, saying, 'Who can ever stop the breeze or the ocean?' He told those who had tried to stop the visit that he had invited a beloved leader to his home for which he needed permission neither from the Maharaja (Hari Singh) nor any of his ministers. Two little girls, my older sisters, were the hostesses because our mother was in purdah. When Panditji arrived, he made them sit next to him and talked to them with great affection. The youngest girl, my third sister, was watching this from a distance. When Panditji eventually took his leave and was getting into his car, she ran out crying, 'When they grow up they will say Panditji took us on his lap and talked to us. What will I say?' Panditji immediately alighted from the car, lifted her up and talked to her for a whole five minutes. On the same trip, when he went to Pahalgam, he bought three necklaces and sent them to my sisters as gifts. They treasured those necklaces for many years. That visit was a milestone in our family's unabashed love for this man.

The first time I met Panditji was in 1952 at a function organized by the irrepressible Shankar Pillai, artist, editor, cartoonist. Let me add here that he made the best cartoons of the prime minister; some of them were collected in a small book which had for its title a remark the 'subject' once made to the cartoonist: 'Don't spare me, Shankar'. Behind this function lies a story which culminated that day. We had moved to Delhi soon after Partition. I was playing in a neighbourhood park when some children coerced me into telling them my name. I use the word 'coerce' deliberately here because I knew instinctively what would happen if I told them my name. So, I tried to avoid saying 'Syeda'. But when they insisted, I mumbled my name, hoping that they would hear it as 'Sarita' and let me go. But they had heard it right. And then came the verdict: 'We won't play with her, she is a Muslim.' This had happened a couple of times before with different groups of kids who played on the lawn. Each time I would go back home ashamed and scared.

The experience became public after I wrote a story, 'You Have to Learn to Make Friends', for *Shankar's Weekly* Children's Number. When it was published, the story went 'viral', as they say in today's terminology, in many parts of the world. It received international acclaim and I became a celebrity overnight! It was beautifully illustrated by an Argentinian artist, Brigitte Frankfurter, who was moved to tears after reading it. Later, Rajkamal Prakashan turned it into a lovely little book and published it in Hindi, Urdu and English. I dedicated the book to Jawaharlal Nehru and Shankar Pillai. Zakir Husain, who later became president of India, wrote the Foreword for the book and the story was reproduced in the *UNESCO Courier*. Khushwant Singh quoted from it in some of his writings and always reminded me that it was my best piece of writing. It was then that I first met the prime minister, who gave me an award at a glittering ceremony that made front-page news. At the awards function I performed a solo play about Peter Rabbit, a favourite tale for kids. When I went to receive the award, I forgot to remove my 'ears'. Nehru smiled and said, 'You have large ears!' Then, handing me a large box, he added, 'This box is bigger than you!' For many decades I treasured the walkie-talkie doll, but much more, those words and the smile that accompanied them.

In his article 'End of an Epoch', Father recalls Nehru's love for children in the very same context: 'The *Shankar's Weekly* was having the annual prize distribution of its international contest in children's writings and paintings and he [Nehru] was invited to preside. As soon as "Chacha Nehru" arrived, a wave of joy and enthusiasm swept through the thousands of children. Nehru surveyed the glittering crowd of diplomats, ministers, government officials and Members of Parliament occupying the front seats and looked displeased: "What is all this? Please go back, all of you, and let the children occupy the seats of honour." He would not rest till the revolutionary "distribution" had been made. And no one minded! Then he was like a child amongst children, playing with them, patting them, rumpling their hair, putting all his garlands around their necks...'

Some special mornings, Father used to take us to PM House for breakfast. In response to his request for a meeting, Nehru always said, '*Nashtey par aa jaao*'—come for breakfast. At the breakfast table I didn't catch the conversation but enjoyed the delicious food and bravely faced his favourite dogs who freely went in and out.

In fact, my family has a treasure house of stories about Panditji. My father's younger sister, Saliha Abid Husain, who was a stalwart of Jamia Millia Islamia, used to often narrate what happened one day in 1947 when there was intense fear in Jamia that the marauders would attack any time. Zakir Husain, who was Shaikh-ul-Jamia (Vice Chancellor) at the time, was extremely worried; that day, he phoned Panditji and spoke just four words: 'This is the end.' With tears in her eyes, Saliha Phupi told me, 'Panditji jumped into a vehicle with only one security guard and ordered the driver to speed. On the way, near Bhogal Market, he saw a crowd with torches. Sensing danger, he jumped out and waving a stick, ran behind the crowd which was trying to set fire to shops owned by Muslims. This is truly the work of a momin [believer in God or Allah].'

*

It was my uncle, the film director, screenwriter and journalist, Khwaja Ahmed Abbas, who had the best fund of stories about Panditji. We would listen to these stories with the same interest as his stories about film stars. Jawaharlal Nehru was our family's brightest star when we were growing up and imbibing the values he imparted to us from time to time through his speeches and writings. K.A. Abbas, as he was known, collected his cherished moments with Panditji and transferred them to three chapters in his autobiography, *I Am Not an Island*. All three chapters had the same title, 'My Long Love Affair'. He recounts how his first memory of Nehru was watching him on screen as a small boy, in a newsreel in Bansal cinema in his hometown, Panipat. On the screen he saw a slim young man riding a white horse. The hall burst into applause. He confesses that even had he been holding the hand of his girlfriend, he would have detached his hand and joined the clapping. 'I said to myself quite irrationally, "This is my leader, my comrade, my beloved."'

This was the start of a relationship that lasted until the very end, the day Nehru died on 27 May 1964.

Abbas recalls the day when he with two fellow students of Aligarh Muslim University jumped onto the train that the prime minister was riding to their alma mater when it stopped at Khurja station. Their purpose was to catch the PM in his cabin before the train reached Aligarh. They spoke for almost an hour; a candid exchange in which both sides spoke from the heart. As the train slowed down he presented his autograph book to his hero. Nehru wrote only two words, 'Live Dangerously, Jawaharlal Nehru'. Abbas inscribed that motto on his heart for the rest of his life.

Abbas's devotion to Nehru made him follow him to Geneva as his 'self-appointed' secretary.

'But I have no money to give you,' Panditji told him.

'I will work for you gratis.'

'But I am against exploiting people.'

Nonetheless, Abbas tagged along with the PM, thanks to some help from Yusuf Meherally, the freedom fighter and mayor of Bombay who was close to Panditji. There in the headquarters of the League of Nations he met the PM who looked peevish and out of sorts. This is what transpired inside the elevator:

'Hello, Abbas.'

'Sir, have you also come to attend the League of Nations?'

'Of course not! Do you think I give any importance to this thieves' kitchen?'

Later he was to meet Panditji at the home of Konni Zilliacus, a friend with whom he was staying. Zilliacus was in the information section of the League of Nations. I had heard this name as a child; he was a friend of my father as well. While they were there, the postman brought mail which the PM eagerly grabbed. It had the packet of newspapers for which he had been waiting. He opened the *National Herald* of which he was chairman. Abbas looked over his shoulder, searching for the article he had sent to the editor about the war scare in Europe. 'Yes, your article is here,' said Nehru. 'But how am I to read it? Shall I stand on my head to know that it was written by Khwaja Ahmed Abbas?' The byline was printed upside down.

Nehru was furious. 'Incompetent! That's what you all are! Can't even bring out a newspaper without silly mistakes.'

'Panditji, I am only the author of this article, not its printer. Why are you getting angry at me?'

The frown was replaced with a smile, then he chuckled, 'Yes, you are right. Why am I shouting at you? Because you are here and the culprits are in Lucknow. Actually, you should have shouted at me. After all, I am chairman of the board of directors and therefore I am responsible.'

That, Abbas wrote, was the wonderful thing about this man—his quick flashes of temper were like storm clouds. When the outburst was over, the horizon would clear with a flashing smile.

Abbas narrated how he was sent on a mission to Kashmir. He met all the leaders and returned to report to his mentor the outcome of his visit. Taking courage, he broached the subject of plebiscite. If the plebiscite is held soon, he told his leader, no more than a handful of Muslim Leaguers would vote for Pakistan. The rest would all opt for India. Nehru reminded Abbas of his commitment before the Constituent Assembly that he would hold the plebiscite as soon as peace and tranquillity returned to the Valley. When Abbas gave many arguments and insisted that the time was now, Nehru shot back, 'Do you want the world to say that India is a liar, that Nehru has gone back on his word? No, Abbas. A plebiscite requires peace and tranquillity for a people to calmly and dispassionately decide between the two alternatives.' Having shot off his mouth before the prime minister of India, Abbas was ready to be thrown out when the PM rang the bell. But when the 'pattewala' came, he said, 'Bring us some tea please.'

Abbas recalls coming out of the meeting shivering slightly in the cold winter air. 'Here was a gentleman in a world of crooks where being a gentleman was dangerous… I could not help admiring and adoring the man who still preferred being a gentleman.'

K.A. Abbas made the first songless film and perhaps the first children's film, *Munna*. On his request, Panditji agreed to view the film in the Rashtrapati Bhavan auditorium. He came late and as he entered he told Abbas, 'I am tired. Don't mind if I fall asleep during the screening.' Abbas took aside the child hero Master Romi and whispered, 'You sit at Panditji's feet. If you see his eyes closing just hold his feet and start crying.' He then sat behind the PM and began to explain the scenes. Panditji snapped, 'Will you be quiet, Abbas, and let me enjoy the film?' As he got up to leave, Abbas asked him for time the next morning. 'Come for breakfast. You and Romi.' What about the others? Abbas asked. 'No, this is only for children,' Panditji replied. Manmohan Krishna, Abbas's dearest friend, professor turned actor and a man with a golden voice, pleaded on behalf of the cast and crew, saying, 'Panditji, we are also your children.' The prime minister turned to his daughter Indira who had accompanied him to the film and asked, 'Indu, are there enough eggs in the house for all of them?'

When Abbas made a film about migrant labour in big cities who are forced to live in large drainpipes, he took brand new faces as the hero and heroine. It had all the ingredients for a box office flop. But it won the President's Gold Medal. Once again Abbas sought an audience with the PM. He divided the award money of 25,000 rupees into cheques of equal amount and placed them in fifteen envelopes for Panditji to present to all the participants. The prime minister was not well that morning, so the doctors had given Abbas only fifteen minutes with him. 'But I had my reservations whether Panditji would let us go so soon,' Abbas writes. While giving the envelope to one of the participants, 'Panditji looked at the cheque and jocularly asked, "I hope Abbas has not committed any arithmetical mistake by dividing the almost indivisible amount [25,000] in fifteen shares." Then he asked, "Isn't there a song in the picture?"' Abbas asked Manmohan Krishna to recite a poem from the film in tarannum (singing or reciting in a musical way). When the last two lines were recited there were tears in many eyes.

Woh jo kho jayein to kho jayegi duniya saari
Woh jo mil jayein to saath apne zamana hoga
(If he goes the whole world will be lost
If he remains all of creation will be with us)

Their time had been up for a long time. When my uncle folded his hands in salutation, Panditji said, 'Why, why? I have no other appointment.'

'As the lift doors closed I saw him smile and wave. I had a premonition that I would never see him again,' wrote my uncle.

⋆

Panditji defined the word jamhooriyat (democracy). This incident was narrated to me by my father. It was Sunday, the 23rd of October, 1955, and thousands of young men and women, participants in the Inter-University Youth Festival, had assembled to listen to their great leader. He arrived punctually, dressed in immaculate khadi, wearing a smile which even shamed the carnation in his buttonhole, sat down, informal and relaxed, on a table (not a chair!), drew the microphone to him and asked: 'Would you like me to talk to you in Hindi or English?' A large majority shouted, 'Hindi'; a minority (from South India mostly) asked for English because they did not follow Hindi. Nehru smiled and said, 'Naturally, you would expect me to honour the democratic majority verdict and speak in Hindi. But do you know what democracy means? A solicitude for the legitimate rights of the minorities and a concern for their needs and welfare. All of you know English but some of your colleagues do not know Hindi. So, I shall speak in English,' adding disarmingly, 'Later, I shall speak briefly in Hindi also.'

Father told us a stunning instance of his fair-mindedness. Once he was travelling on the same flight as Nehru from India to England and on the way the plane stopped at Cairo. 'It was about 1 a.m. He made his way to the lounge where he found himself surrounded by press reporters who had got wind of his passing through. They started asking him questions, many of them about the disputes between India and Pakistan, Kashmir, canal waters, settlement of evacuee property, and so on. Nehru answered them patiently, reasonably, with good humour. Several times, after stating India's stand firmly and clearly, he would pause and say, "But you know Pakistan has its own point of view about it." He then proceeded to explain it as fairly as possible. I have never known a politician doing so in any major dispute, except when he was merely anxious to demolish the other side's argument!'

In his Jawaharlal Nehru Memorial Lecture, Father recalled another characteristic which is unimaginable today. 'I remember a small incident which throws revealing light on his approach to things. There is in Delhi an old, historic wall which used to run round the whole of the city and parts of which are still standing. The Municipal Corporation had decided to demolish it—in fact, part of it had actually been demolished—in order, forsooth, to release some land it could profitably rent out. No one had raised any objection or perhaps even noticed it. Driving along the Bahadur Shah Zafar Marg one day Nehru happened to see this act of vandalism and immediately the famous Nehru temper came into operation. He sharply admonished the persons responsible and ordered the demolition to be stopped.'

On 24 October 1955 my father, then Secretary, Ministry of Education, wrote a letter to the PM suggesting that he address the youth of the nation every month. He referred to Nehru's talk at the Inter-University Youth Festival the previous evening. 'While I listened to you…the public address had the appeal and intimacy of a fireside chat.' He urged Nehru to speak to the youth every month. 'I know that…it would be impossible for you to find time for this but if I may say so, when have you abided by the normal laws of time?' Panditji liked the suggestion but could never put it into practice—even he, it seems, could not circumvent the laws of time. And so we had to wait decades for 'Mann ki Baat' to happen, albeit with a very different prime minister!

*

Another close family member who told us about Panditji was my uncle Syed Abid Husain. He was one of the triumvirate who with Zakir Husain and Mohammad Mujeeb founded Jamia Millia. Breakfast with Nehru was when their meetings took place. Once when he reached the PM House, Panditji was walking in the garden. Abid being an avid walker, joined him and recited to him a quatrain he had composed on Kalu Lal Shrimali, the man who succeeded Maulana Azad as education minister. Panditji chuckled, he liked Abid Sahib's wry humour and asked him to write it down in his famous red diary. '*Janab e baghbaan jinko shri maali bhi kehte hain,*' Abid began writing. 'You are too slow, give it to me,' said Nehru impatiently. Abid was surprised at his knowledge of Urdu. 'Snatching the diary from my hand, Panditji wrote even as he was walking.'

He once confessed, with a naiveté and frankness which were so endearing: 'I have become a queer mixture of the East and West, out of place everywhere, at home nowhere… I am a stranger and alien in the West. I cannot be of it. But in my country also, sometimes, I have an exile's feeling.' Father writes in his autobiography that history will record that Nehru was predominantly a world citizen, equally at home in the East and the West. What he really meant was that he could not identify himself exclusively, much less aggressively with either, that he saw things to appreciate and admire as well as condemn and criticize in both.

Talking about the avid Nehru-denigrators and critics, Father writes that the man remained untouched, unembittered by all this persecution and inhuman treatment which would have seared the soul and been the moral undoing of most other men. He fought the British government in India with a lion's courage and singleness of purpose but his admiration for their language and literature, science and technology, social and political ideas and many traits of their character remained unaffected. And when the time came for political settlement with them, under the inspiration of Gandhi, he behaved with a grace and largeness of heart which has few parallels in history. To quote a Greek poet:

I was running a race with the Reaper.
I hastened; he lingered; I won.
Now, strike, Death! You sluggard, you sleeper,
You cannot undo what I have done.

*

Since most of my life's work has been on Maulana Azad, I want to end this piece of writing with what Nehru said in his Azad Memorial Lecture on 11 November 1958, the year that Azad passed away:

> 'I want India to advance on the material plane, to fulfil her Five-Year Plans, to raise the standard of living of her vast population; I want the narrow conflicts of today in the name of religion and caste, language or province, to cease and a classless and casteless society to be built up, where every individual has full opportunity to grow according to his worth and ability. In particular, I hope that the curse of caste will be ended for there cannot be either democracy or socialism on the basis of caste…
>
> 'I have no doubt that India will progress industrially and otherwise, that she will advance in science and technology, that our people's standards will rise, that education will spread and that health conditions will be better and that art and culture will enrich the people's lives. We have started on this pilgrimage with strong purpose and good heart and we shall reach the end of the journey, however long that may be…

> But what I am concerned with is not merely our material progress but the quality and depth of our people. Gaining power through industrial processes, will they lose themselves in the quest of individual wealth and soft living? That would be a tragedy, for it would be a negation of what India has stood for in the past and, I think, in the present times also, as exemplified by Gandhi, power is necessary but wisdom is essential. It is only power with wisdom that is good... Can we combine the progress of science and technology with this purpose of the mind and the spirit also? We cannot be untrue to science because that represents the basic feat of life today. Still less can we be untrue to those essential principles for which India has stood throughout the ages. Let us then pursue our path to industrial progress with all our strength and vigour and at the same time remember that industrial riches, without toleration and compassion and wisdom, may well turn to dust and ashes. Let us also remember that "blessed are the peacemakers".'

Finally, in his own picturesque words,

> 'Life is rich and varied and though it has many swamps and marshes and muddy places, it has the great sea, and the mountains, and snow and glaciers, and wonderful starlit nights, and the love of family and friends, and the comradeship of workers in a common cause, and music and books and the empire of ideas. So that each one of us may well say:

> Lord, though I lived on earth, the child of earth,
> Yet was I fathered by the starry sky.
>
> 'I am not wedded to any dogma or religion. But I do believe—whether one calls it religion or not—in the innate spirituality of human beings. I do believe in the innate dignity of the individual.
>
> 'I am proud of that great inheritance that has been, and is, ours, and I am conscious that I too, like all of us, am a link in that unbroken chain which goes back in the dawn of history in the immemorial past of India. That chain I would not break, for I treasure it and seek inspiration from it. And, as witness of this desire of mine and as my last homage to India's cultural inheritance, I am making the request that a handful of my ashes should be thrown into the Ganga at Allahabad to be carried to the great ocean that washes India's shores.'

I have a book of poems which were written as a tribute to Nehru by Urdu poets after he passed away. (The book was called *Amar Jyot* and was published in 1965, priced at Rs 2.) Urdu was everyone's language, Hindus as well as Muslims, which is why half the poems in this book are by Hindu poets.

Hiralal 'Falak' Dehlavi wrote these lines which generations should remember for many reasons including the play on words which is unfortunately lost in the English translation:

> *Woh sidq e dil se ahl e watan ko qubool hain*
> *Moti ke laal ke jo sunehri usool hain*

Ab aur bhi hui hai muqaddas ye sarzameen
Gang o Jaman ki goad mein Nehru ke phool hain
(Our watan accepts with sincerity
Golden principles of this jewel of moti
This region is even more sacred because
In the lap of Ganga-Jamuna lie his ashes)

Today, the rulers of India are wondering what to do with us Muslims, a population of 200 million. As a Muslim brought up under the protective aura of the triumvirate of Gandhi-Nehru-Azad I have caught myself saying, Why am I here? Where do I belong? If my elders could hear me from *bahisht* (paradise) they would cringe at this question. Panditji would also glare at me along with my ancestors.

But what is happening today? The former Union Minister for Tourism, Mahesh Sharma, visits the family of Ravi Sisodia who lynched Mohammed Akhlaq in Dadri; another former minister, Jayant Sinha, garlands eight people convicted of lynching Afrazul, a Muslim cattle trader from Bengal; the prime minister hosts a felicitation for social media trolls including one best known for celebrating the murder of journalist Gauri Lankesh; party men march in support of the rapists and murderers of an eight-year-old child in Kathua. I could go on but will stop at Bilkis Bano, the mutilation of whose family in Limkheda was in my 'eyescape' when I went there in March 2002. Today, the perpetrators of the crimes against Bilkis Bano and her family walk free.

In these days of divisiveness, polarization, intolerance, what is happening in Kashmir and to Muslims, Jawaharlal Nehru rises before my eyes. Icon, symbol, emblem.

About the Contributors

Purushottam Agrawal is a writer, academic and political commentator. He was formerly a professor at the Centre of Indian Languages, School of Language, Literature and Culture Studies, Jawaharlal Nehru University, of which he later also served as chairman. From 2007 to 2013 he was a member of the Union Public service Commission. He specializes in Bhakti poetry and its social context (especially that of Kabir) and has written books on literary criticism as well as academic papers in both English and Hindi. He is the author of *Padmavat: An Epic Love Story* (2018) and *Kabir, Kabir: The Life and Work of the Early Modern Poet-Philosopher* (2021), and editor of *'Who is Bharat Mata?': On History, Culture and the Idea of India: Writings By and On Jawaharlal Nehru* (2019). He contributes regularly to newspapers and magazines on a wide range of cultural and political issues.

Mani Shankar Aiyar is a former diplomat turned politician, who after a distinguished foreign service career became a senior leader in the Indian National Congress (Congress Party). Aiyar entered the Indian Foreign Service (IFS) in 1963, and over the next fifteen years served at various overseas diplomatic missions, including Belgium, North Vietnam and Iraq. In 1978, he was named India's first consul general to Pakistan, a portfolio he held until 1982.

Between 1982 and 1989, Aiyar was joint secretary, ministry

of external affairs (MEA), as well as joint secretary to the prime minister (1985-89). In 1989, Aiyar retired from the foreign service to pursue a career in politics. As a member of the Congress Party, he served as special assistant to Rajiv Gandhi, who was then president of the party, until Gandhi's assassination in 1991. His proximity to the Gandhi family shaped much of his subsequent political career.

During his tenure in the UPA government, Aiyar held the portfolios for the ministries of Panchayati Raj, petroleum and natural gas, youth affairs and sports, and development of the North-eastern region. In 2006 he was honoured as the year's outstanding parliamentarian by the President of India.

In March 2010, he was nominated to the Rajya Sabha by the President on the strength of his expertise in the field of social services and his literary accomplishments. As a member of the Rajya Sabha, he served on the Standing Committee on Rural Development and on the Consultative Committee on External Affairs.

Aiyar is also a skilled orator, a prolific newspaper and journal columnist, and an authority on South Asian politics. His books include *Remembering Rajiv* (1992), *Pakistan Papers* (1994), *Knickerwallahs, Silly-Billies and Other Curious Creatures* (1995), *Confessions of a Secular Fundamentalist* (2004), and *A Time of Transition: Rajiv Gandhi to the 21st Century* (2009).

Hartosh Singh Bal is the political editor at *The Caravan* magazine, and an adjunct faculty member at the Jindal School of Journalism & Communication. He is the author of *Waters Close Over Us: A Journey Along the Narmada*. He was formerly political editor at *Open* magazine.

Rakesh Batabyal teaches history at the Centre for Media Studies in the School of Social Science, Jawaharlal Nehru University where he has been the deputy director and associate professor of the UGC Academic Staff College since 2000. Dr Batabyal was the Inaugural India Chair Professor, Tokyo University in

2010 and has also been a Fellow of the National Institute of Punjab Studies and of the Indian Institute of Advanced Study, Shimla (1996-99). He has taught at the University of Kelaniya, Sri Lanka, and has earned his diploma in Romanian language from University of Bucharest.

Dr Batabyal is the author of several books including *Communalism in Bengal: From Famine to Noakhali (1943-47)*, Sage Publications, Delhi, Thousand Oaks and London, April 2005; *The Penguin Book of Modern Indian Speeches* (ed.), Penguin Books India, July 2007; *JNU: The Making of A University*, HarperCollins Publishers India, 2014; and *Building a Free India* (ed.), Speaking Tiger, July 2022.

Neera Chandhoke is Distinguished Fellow at the Centre for Equity Studies, New Delhi. She was formerly Professor of Political Science and Director of the Developing Countries Research Centre at the University of Delhi. She is the author of several notable books on the culture and politics of contemporary India including *State and Civil Society: Explorations in Political Theory* (1995), *Beyond Secularism: Rights of Religious Minorities* (1999), *Contested Secessions: Rights, Self-determination, Democracy, and Kashmir* (2011) and *Rethinking Pluralism, Secularism and Tolerance: Anxieties of Coexistence* (2019).

Gopalkrishna Gandhi is a former civil servant and diplomat who served as the Governor of West Bengal from 2004 to 2009. He joined the Indian Administrative Service (IAS) in 1968 and served in Tamil Nadu till 1985, when he became secretary to the Vice-President of India (1985-87), and thereafter joint secretary to the President of India (1987-92).

In 1992 he became minister (culture) in the Indian high commission in the United Kingdom, and director of the Nehru Centre in London. This was followed by various diplomatic and administrative positions including high commissioner of India to South Africa and Lesotho (1996); secretary to the President of India (1997-2000); high commissioner to Sri Lanka (2000), and ambassador to Norway and Iceland (2002).

He is the author of one novel, *Saranam* (Refuge) and a play in verse, *Dara Shukoh*. His other books are *Gandhi and South Africa* (co-edited with E.S. Reddy), *Koi Accha Sa Ladka* (a translation into Hindustani of Vikram Seth's novel, *A Suitable Boy*), *Gandhi and Sri Lanka*, *Nehru and Sri Lanka*, *The Oxford India Gandhi* and *A Frank Friendship/Gandhi and Bengal: A Descriptive Chronology* (compiled and edited).

He is currently Distinguished Professor of History and Politics, Ashoka University.

Ramachandra Guha is a historian and environmentalist. He is widely regarded as one of the foremost authorities on the history of modern India. In 2011–12, he held a visiting position at the London School of Economics, where he occupied the Philippe Roman Chair in History and International Affairs. In 2019, the American Historical Association conferred its Honorary Foreign Member prize on Guha. He has also been a visiting professor at the Indian Institute of Science, Bengaluru. Among his numerous publications are the three commercially successful and critically acclaimed books on modern India: *India After Gandhi* (2007), *Gandhi Before India* (2013) and *Gandhi: The Years That Changed the World* (2018). He has also written a history of Indian cricket *A Corner of a Foreign Field: The Indian History of a British Sport* (2002) as well as a book on global environmental thought and action, *Environmentalism: A Global History* (2014). He is a regular contributor to various newspapers and academic journals.

Syeda Hameed is a women's rights activist, educationist and writer. She is a former member of the Planning Commission of India as well as a member of the National Commission for Women. She also served as chancellor of the Maulana Azad National Urdu University, Hyderabad until 2015. She has authored and edited translations as well as books on Islam, Sufism, gender and development. Her publications include books on Muslim social leaders of India like *Islamic Seal on India's*

Independence: Abul Kalam Azad—A Fresh Look (1998) and *Dr Zakir Husain: Teacher Who Became President* (2000). She is the founder trustee of the Women's Initiative for Peace in South Asia, and a member of the Delhi-based think-tank Centre for Dialogue and Reconciliation. In 2006, the Al-Ameen Educational Society of Bengaluru awarded her their Al-Ameen All India Community Leadership Award. The following year, the Government of India conferred the fourth highest civilian award, the Padma Shri, on Hameed for her service to Indian society.

Shabnam Hashmi is a social and human rights activist based in Delhi. She has been a leading campaigner against communalism in India in the last two decades and has worked extensively with victims of the Gujarat riots of 2002 in particular. She is the founder of the non-profit socio-cultural organization Act Now for Harmony and Democracy (ANHAD). She was awarded the Association for Communal Harmony in Asia (ACHA) Star Award for Communal Harmony in 2005, the Aamil Smriti Samman in 2005 and the National Minority Rights Award 2008 by the National Minority Commission.

Kumar Ketkar is a senior journalist and former chief editor of leading Marathi dailies *Maharashtra Times* and *Loksatta*. He has also been special correspondent of *The Economic Times* and resident editor, *The Observer* of Politics and Economy. Currently, he is the chief editor of *Dainik Divya Marathi*. He is the author of twelve books in Marathi on politics, sociology and literary criticism. A regular TV commentator, he also serves as a media consultant with a TV channel, Mi Marathi. He was nominated to the Rajya Sabha from Maharashtra in March 2018.

Aditya Mukherjee is Professor of Contemporary Indian History, Centre for Historical Studies, and Dean, School of Social Sciences, Jawaharlal Nehru University (JNU), New Delhi. He was educated at St Stephen's College and JNU. He is the Editor of the Sage Series in Modern Indian History published by Sage Publications, (sixteen monographs already published) and was editor of the *Selected Works of Jawaharlal Nehru* (2009-11). He was Member of The Indian Council for Historical Research (ICHR) from 2009-15 and is currently Member, Executive Council, Indian History Congress. He specializes in economic history, particularly business history and the political economy of post-colonial development. He was president of the Indian History Congress for Modern India, 2007-8. He has been Visiting Professor at Duke University, USA, 1986; JSPS fellow and Japan Foundation Fellow at University of Tokyo, Japan, 1996 and 1999-2000 respectively; Visiting Fellow at the Institutes of Advanced Study at Lancaster, UK, and at the University of Sao Paulo, Brazil; Fellow at the Institute of Advanced Study at Nantes, France, 2010 and Visiting Professor at La Sapienza, University of Rome, Italy, 2013. His publications include the following books: *India's Struggle for Independence*, Viking, 1988, Penguin, 1989, 58th reprint in 2014, and *India Since Independence*, Penguin, 2008, both co-authored and translated into five languages; *Imperialism, Nationalism and the Making of the Indian Capitalist Class 1927-1947*, Sage, 2002; *RSS, School Texts and the Murder of Mahatma Gandhi: The Hindu Communal Project*, Sage, 2008, co-author; *A Centenary History of the Indian National Congress, 1964-1984, Vol. V*, editor, Academic Publishers, New Delhi, 2011.

Mridula Mukherjee is Professor of Modern Indian History at the Centre for Historical Studies, Jawaharlal Nehru University (JNU), New Delhi. She has been the Director of the Nehru Memorial Museum and Library, President of the Indian History Congress (Modern India), Dean, School of Social Sciences, JNU and has edited the *Selected Works of Jawaharlal Nehru*. She is the editor of the Sage Series in Modern Indian History (sixteen monographs already published). She specializes in agrarian history, peasant movements, the Indian national movement and Gandhi. She has been a Visiting Scholar at Duke University, USA, and University of Tokyo, Japan, and a Visiting Fellow at the Nantes Institute of Advanced Study, France, and at the Institutes of Advanced Study at Lancaster, UK, and Sao Paulo, Brazil, and Visiting Professor at La Sapienza, The University of Rome, Italy. She has co-authored two best-selling books called *India's Struggle for Independence*, Penguin, 1989 (more than fifty reprints by 2014) and *India Since Independence*, Penguin, 2008 (both translated into several languages). Her other publications are *Peasants in India's Non-violent Revolution, Practice and Theory*, Sage Publications, 2004 and *Colonializing Agriculture: The Myth of Punjab Exceptionalism*, Sage Publications, 2006 and *RSS, School Texts and the Murder of Mahatma Gandhi: The Hindu Communal Project*, Sage Publications, 2008.

Kiran Nagarkar (1942-2019) was a novelist, playwright, film and drama critic and screenwriter both in Marathi and English, and one of the most significant writers of post-colonial India.

Amongst his most known works are *Saat Sakkam Trechalis* (Seven Sixes Are Forty Three) (1974), *Ravan and Eddie* (1994), the epic novel, *Cuckold* (1997) for which he was awarded the 2001 Sahitya Akademi Award in English,*God's Little Soldier* (2006), *The Extras* (2012) and the highly controversial play, *Bedtime Story*.

Nagarkar's last book, *The Arsonist*, a fictionalized account of the life of the Bhakti saint-poet Kabir, was published in 2019.

Aakar Patel is a writer and columnist, and rights activist based in Bangalore. He has served as the head of Amnesty International in India (2015-19) and currently serves as the Chair of the Board of Amnesty International in India. He is a former newspaper editor and has worked at publications across India. *Why I Write*, Patel's book translating Saadat Hasan Manto's non-fiction from Urdu to English was published in 2014. He has authored two more books since, *Our Hindu Rashtra* (2020) and *Price of the Modi Years* (2021), on the rise of Hindu majoritarianism and the Narendra Modi government since 2014, respectively.

Shiv Visvanathan is a social scientist best known for his contributions to developing the field of science and technology studies, and for the concept of cognitive justice, a term he coined. He is currently Professor at OP Jindal Global University, Sonepat. Prior to this, he was Professor, Dhirubhai Ambani Institute of Information and Communication Technology (DA-IICT), in Gandhinagar, Gujarat, and has held the position of Senior Fellow, Centre for the Study of Developing Societies (CSDS) in Delhi. He has also taught at the Delhi School of Economics and held visiting professorships in the US at Smith College, Stanford, Goldsmiths, and Arizona State University, and at Maastricht University in the Netherlands. He is the author of *Organizing for Science* (OUP, Delhi, 1985), *A Carnival for Science* (OUP, Delhi, 1997) and has co-edited *Foulplay: Chronicles of Corruption* (Banyan Books, Delhi, 1999).

Professor Visvanathan is a regular columnist in newspapers like *The Hindu, The New Indian Express, Indian Express, The Deccan Chronicle* and *The Asian Age*. He also contributes to popular magazines like *Outlook, India Today, Governance Today* and *Tehelka*. His popular writings touch topics as wide-ranging as science, cricket, anthropology, development, intellectual history, and walking.

ALSO FROM SPEAKING TIGER

BUILDING A FREE INDIA

Defining Speeches of Our Independence Movement That Shaped the Nation

Edited by Rakesh Batabyal

'Start reading this book and you will return to it in your darkest hour.' —Aditi Phadnis, *Business Standard*

India's democratic ethos was a product of the foundational ideas of our freedom movement. As the movement progressed—from the economic critique of colonial rule by the early nationalists, to the unequivocal demand for Purna Swaraj and the immense moral authority of the Mahatma Gandhi-led resistance—the notion of an equal society that ensured dignity to all—irrespective of caste, class, gender or religion—came to occupy a central place in it. By the time the Constituent Assembly met in December 1946, not just civil rights, but the particular rights of women, of minorities, of the Depressed Classes and the Adivasis were being publicly articulated and demanded, not as favours but as a matter of course.

Building a Free India brings together landmark speeches delivered over roughly a century by the leading lights of the national movement—from Dadabhai Naoroji, Surendranath Banerjee, Bhikaiji Cama, Lajpat Rai and Tilak, to Gandhi, Nehru, Ambedkar, Bose, Sarojini Naidu and Maulana Azad—as well as a range of lesser-known but equally remarkable figures. This unprecedented collection is not only an invaluable history of our freedom movement but also of the ideas of universal equality, dignity and justice that are—and must always remain—at the root of our democracy.

ALSO FROM SPEAKING TIGER

'WHO IS BHARAT MATA?'

On History, Culture and the Idea of India
Writings by and on Jawaharlal Nehru

Edited by Purushottam Agrawal

'A timely volume which will also stand the test of time.'
—Rudrangshu Mukherjee, *The Hindu*

'Who is Bharat Mata, whose victory you wish?' asked Jawaharlal Nehru—a leading light of the Indian freedom movement who would become the country's first prime minister—at a public gathering in 1936. And then he explained: the mountains and rivers, forests and fields were of course dear to everyone, but what counted ultimately were 'the people of India—spread out all over this vast land.' This collection of writings and speeches by and on Nehru shows us the mind—the ideology, born of experience, observation and deep study—behind this democratic and inclusive idea of India. It is a book of particular relevance at a time when 'nationalism' and the slogan 'Bharat Mata ki Jai' are being used to construct a militant and purely emotional idea of India that excludes millions of residents and citizens.

'Who Is Bharat Mata?' contains selections from Nehru's classic books—*An Autobiography*, *Glimpses of World History* and *The Discovery of India*; his speeches, essays and letters from the pre- and post-Independence years; and some of his most revealing interviews. The concluding section of the book comprises reminiscences and assessments of Nehru by his contemporaries—among them, Mahatma Gandhi, Bhagat Singh, Sardar Patel, Maulana Azad, Aruna Asaf Ali, Sheikh Abdullah, Ramdhari Singh Dinkar, Ali Sardar Jafri, Martin Luther King Jr and Atal Bihari Vajpayee.